THE
INJURY-FREE
HORSE

Hands-on Methods for Maintaining Soundness & Health

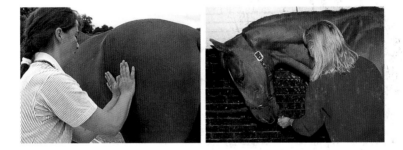

AMANDA SUTTON

Photography by Bob Langrish

Trafalgar Square Publishing

DISCLAIMER

This book is not diagnostic, and has not been written to substitute or replace your vet, farrier or physiotherapist, or any person in your support team; it is to give you a greater understanding of your role in maintaining a pain-free, healthy horse. If anywhere I have written something that does not support your present advice, then always discuss it with your veterinary surgeon. All horses are individuals, and every one slightly different. It should be used whenever possible on an injury-free animal. Where you have a diagnosed problem, discuss the merits of this book with those in charge of the horse's recovery, and they can advise you of its appropriateness.

Take great care in performing any of the 'hands-on' techniques or schooling exercises, and seek advice from your physiotherapist or trainer if you experience any problems. The horse can be an unpredictable animal, so do not put yourself in a vulnerable position.

First published in the United States of America in 2001 by
Trafalgar Square Publishing, North Pomfret, Vermont 05053

Printed in Italy by Stige SpA

All photographs by Bob Langrish except those listed on page 160
All artworks by Maggie Raynor except those listed on page 160

Text copyright © Amanda Sutton 2001
Photographs copyright © David & Charles 2001 except pp 9 (left), 60 (top left), 68 (btm), 113, 115, 138 (btm), 143, 145 (btm), 147 (both), 150, 151, 152, 153, 154
Artworks copyright © David & Charles 2001

ISBN 1-57076-199-X
Library of Congress Catalog Card: 2001086859

Foreword

Amanda Sutton runs Harestock Stud, a physiotherapy centre dedicated to the care and healing of animals. Amanda has a unique perspective relating to horses and their owners, due to her fourteen years of experience in animal physiotherapy. She has been active in ACPAT – the Association of Chartered Physiotherapists in Animal Therapy – since its conception eleven years ago.

I met Amanda several years ago when she agreed to provide training to physical therapists and veterinarians in the United States. She offered expert advice as therapists in our country began to develop an animal physical therapy group within the American Physical Therapy Association. Amanda and I collaborated to provide the keynote address for the First International Conference on Rehabilitation and Physical Therapy in Veterinary Medicine. Veterinary and physical therapy professionals from around the world met in Corvallis, Oregon to share research and intervention strategies for the benefit of all animals. This organisation, through the efforts of many dedicated professionals including Amanda, will contribute to the future of physical rehabilitation for animals.

In keeping with this perspective of sharing information and benefiting animals on a global basis, I am honoured to comment on this innovative and thorough guide to *The Injury-Free Horse*. We live in an era where preventive health care is a necessity, not just a passing phase. We must take an active role in decisions about medical treatments and learn to look for signs of impending problems rather than waiting for symptoms to become serious. This approach is true for human and veterinary medicine.

In my experience in the United States, and I suspect many other countries, horse owners are sometimes unsure when dealing with health issues. They may ask themselves: Whom should I contact for this problem? What do I need to tell the veterinarian? The physical therapist? The farrier? Is what I am seeing a serious problem? What treatment might be helpful? What can I do to help? Amanda has written a simple self-help guide that will help owners find the answers to these questions.

Knowledge is a powerful tool. Through using this guide, owners can easily learn how to look for signs of injury, it will help them become more aware of the significance of abnormal movement and imbalance, and to understand the rationale for various interventions. The role of nutrition, training equipment and tack, and complementary therapies are addressed as well.

By using the simple procedures of massage, stretching, exercise and suppling on a routine basis, you will come to *know your horse*. *You* will know when something is not normal. *You* will know whom to call and when to call. *You* will be able to help maximise your horse's performance. *You* will be able to offer more comfort to your horse. *You* now have the tools you need to make a difference in your horse's life and health.

I believe that this book is the best gift you could give yourself and your horse in whatever equestrian discipline you participate in.

LIN MCGONAGLE, MSPT, LVT
Past President and founding member of the
Animal Physical Therapist SIG,
American Physical Therapy Association.
Author of *Animal Physical Therapy Resource Manual*

DEDICATION

To my children, Ella and Daniel, and husband Ian, with all my love.

ACKNOWLEDGEMENTS

It would have been impossible to have written this book without the people around me, who have both supported and advised me. My work colleagues have been a very special group who have tolerated and put up with the endless turmoil that inevitably a book of this nature creates. A special mention should be made to Joyce, Sandy and Ian who all helped make deadlines and deciphered endless amounts of handwriting.

I have been so lucky to have learnt from many generous people, but feel a deep sense of gratitude to Janet Ellis. She was, and still is, very inspirational, and instilled in me a sense of loyalty and respect for these wonderful animals. I only hope that we will all continue to learn, and thereby benefit the horse as a result.

Success is about teamwork and this has been no more apparent than in the working relationship with William and Wiggy Fox-Pitt that I have been so fortunate to have. Their commitment to providing the very best of care and their professionalism has resulted in a most desirable environment in which to be involved. Their commitment to their horses and their help with this book has been fantastic.

My family continue to provide great guidance and tolerance, especially my husband Ian. It takes so many people to work together and although it is never easy, with great highs and lows, you cannot carry on if you do not believe in what you are doing or have the support of those around you. My parents, sisters and Ian have far outdone themselves on this score. Thank you.

Contents

6–32

33–48

49–76

77–112

113–142

143–160

Introduction

INTRODUCTION

In human medicine we have effectively battled against many of the old enemies such as infectious disease, but now we have others, and in the main these are thought to be stress related. Diet and exercise play a very significant part in their manifestation, and in a world where we spend much of our time sitting or driving, working, watching television, or playing computer games, it is not difficult to understand how such problems arise. The stresses are often related to our social or work environments, involving perhaps divorce, finance or work. In moderation, stress gives us the drive to get things done; but in excess it is counter-

Farrier, vet and physiotherapist working together: a multi-discipline approach will help to maximise your horse's performance

productive, and leads to illness and injury as a result of its knock-on effects on our bodies.

Such a sedentary life-style, so singularly lacking in variety of movement, and today's stress levels, all throw our muscular system totally out of balance. We simply do not move enough. In order to reverse this trend, to help us 'uncoil' and lengthen out, and to prevent damaging effects on our self-repairing capacity, we need exercise.

Horses, like ourselves, are exposed to risk all day. Obvious hazards can be removed; or if you are aware of more subtle signs of change in your horse, you can ensure that he does not continue working with a problem, thereby causing long-term damage.

For both rider and horse, in order to reduce the risk of injury you must have an

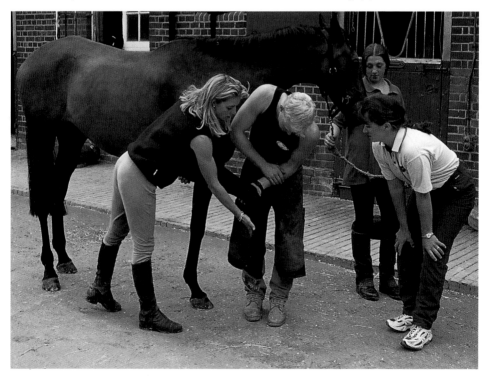

understanding of how injuries happen, and how they can be avoided. Unfortunately not all risks are foreseeable and accidents do happen; moreover, some areas within equestrianism carry a higher risk, such as eventing or steeplechasing. One way to avoid traumatic injuries is to reduce the risk factors, creating a safe working environment and minimising the chance of accidents, and by the regular maintenance of sporting equipment and tack.

Overuse injuries can also be avoided, by allowing the body time to adapt to repetitive stress. Any sudden change in training routine – yours or the horse – will cause a deleterious 'knock-on' effect in both your bodies. We cannot suddenly undertake a strenuous exercise regime without risk: it has to be a gradual process, building up in easy stages

To maintain flexibility and prevent injury, it is essential that both of you are always thoroughly warmed up before exercise, and completely cooled down – a process known as 'warming down' – at the end of it: returning the body to its normal temperature is important so as to avoid stiffness later.

Common sense and self discipline in knowing when to stop exercise, and when not to start it, are important for avoiding any kind of injury. Illness, fatigue, pain and stiffness are warnings that your horse or yourself should not be taking exercise: you have to know how much to do, how to build it up safely, and how to be specific for your horse's requirements.

This book teaches you to observe your horse in a way that you have not done before, and to identify and remedy problems that will cause loss of performance in your horse.

'Warming down' at the Atlanta Olympics was vital if the horse was to maintain his maxiumum performance ability next day

Introduction

Each horse and rider or driver comprises an individual team, and their exercise regime needs to be designed with their specific requirements in mind. The following points are important in determining the type and method of exercise.

Horse
- breed
- conformation
- age
- previous exercise history
- level of fitness now
- previous injuries
- level of competition
- timing of competition

Rider/Driver
- ability
- objectives
- time

Environment
- weather
- terrain
- facilities

The horse's age and its previous history as related to exercise will both significantly affect the rate of progress possible to achieve fitness. Thus for a young horse starting for the first time on an exercise plan, progress must be slow to allow adequate time for its frame – ligaments, tendons, cartilage and bone – to adapt to the stresses placed upon it. Thoroughbred horses show the most rapid cardiovascular adaptability to exercise, whereas warmbloods require much more work to reach the same level of fitness. The temperament of the horse will also have an effect on how his fitness is increased because of the way he responds and the approach required from the handler. Furthermore, if the horse has had an injury in the past, then it

will be very important to incorporate appropriate strength training and specific suppling exercise in order to return the injured part to full function.

In preparing the horse for competition you will use a regime that combines conditioning and schooling. As a result of conditioning, there will be physiological and structural changes within the horse's body which allow for maximum performance and the maintenance of soundness; and by schooling your horse you develop neuromuscular co-ordination and mental discipline. Thus a well conditioned and schooled horse is one that is both mentally and physically fit, and fully prepared for its job.

Left: A waterlogged main arena at the Atlanta Olympics 1996 – such dramatic changes in terrain can make great demands on the horse's fitness

Right: For maximum performance cardio-vascular conditioning is of paramount importance for the racehorse

Far right: Dynamic suppling exercises improve joint mobility

THE CONDITIONING PROCESS

This includes cardiovascular conditioning, strength training and suppling exercises. A conditioning programme is necessary in order to increase fitness levels.

Steps to the Conditioning Process

1 Low intensity exercise in early stages, of increasing duration.
2 Maintain or decrease duration as the intensity of the exercise is increased.
3 Sport specific: the duration of the exercise periods and the rest intervals is dictated by the discipline.

How frequently you have to exercise in order to improve fitness depends on how much exercise is done in each session. It is very important to have sufficient recovery time between each session to allow the tissues themselves to recover, because if exercised too frequently the risk of injury will be increased due to their being overloaded. The terrain itself also affects the effort expended or energy utilised; for instance, working on a gradient or in deep going will increase the exercise intensity, and so will working in hot and humid conditions.

To improve fitness it is recommended to follow a regime of cardiovascular and strength training sessions two or three times a week with a day's light work in between; for maintaining fitness, one to two sessions per week should be sufficient. Suppling exercises, on the other hand, can be carried out daily in the maintenance of fitness.

In order to prevent injury in ourselves and our horses we must also be aware of any limitations caused by lifestyle or previous injury, and by our own and the horse's inherent ability; and so we should always plan a programme based on cardiovascular and muscular requirements identifying potential risk factors along the way such as overloading, fatigue and terrain.

ACTION	EFFECTS
Cardiovascular conditioning.	Respiratory, cardiovascular and muscular systems will be better able to produce energy correctly.
Strength training.	Improves the power and endurance of muscle groups.
Suppling exercises.	Increases the range of motion of joints. Enhances athleticism. Improves the quality of work. Reduces the risk of injury.

Introduction

INTRODUCTION

If your horse is injured, his exercise will be cut back, and for a competition horse his targets adjusted accordingly. Inevitably injury involves time off work, and financial considerations might include veterinary diagnosis and treatment, remedial shoeing, physiotherapy, management changes (different feed or bedding) and lost entry fees. If the injury is diagnosed early enough, then hopefully there will be minimal secondary effects; but if it is not, it may become more complex, and may result in an overuse strain with all its compensatory problems. Then the recovery period is even longer, and more time is lost, and what is more, the overall value of your animal will almost certainly be reduced due to his decreased performance capacity.

If your horse is at livery or boarded out, the riding time lost can cause considerable financial discomfort and resentment – and when specialist rehabilitation is required, costs can escalate beyond all proportion. Injury requires professional management and care, and this is expensive – and leaving recovery to nature is not a cheaper alternative, because although nature heals, it is not with a view to a full functional return to the level of work prior to injury. Time off from work, veterinary visits and transportation costs all mount up – but they create a burden that is not always necessary. This is because a correct exercise routine that leads to the fitness levels required by the horse for him to do his job will mean less likelihood of strain on the musculo-skeletal system. The end result is a happy, mobile and injury-free horse.

The most common avoidable injuries, and their probable causes, are laid out below.

AVOIDABLE INJURY	PROBABLE CAUSE
Soft tissue strain, such as tendons, ligaments.	Insufficient strength because of insufficient training for the level of effort demanded.
	Insufficient flexibility because of insufficient training or exercise.
	Poor nutrition and proprioception from lack of correct exercise.
	Excessive strain as a result of incorrect bio-mechanics, *ie* faulty foot balance, decreased stride length as a result of shoulder and/or spinal problem (compensatory or primary).
Muscle injuries.	Insufficient warm-up.
	Not adequately mobilised.
	Not trained to the level of exercise/competition demanded.
	Decreased function caused by fibrosed tissue resulting from previous injury.
	Secondary problems resulting from torsional strains or direct injury, or in compensation for primary problems elsewhere.
Bone injuries, such as splints, shin soreness, joint damage.	Faulty training programme.
	Poor environmental factors, such as hard, unlevel going.
	Gait abnormality causing excessive loading.
	Joint damage from decreased support of soft tissues and decreased sensory input.

Evaluation of the Normal Horse

What is normal? Many of us have a contented horse who does what we ask of him in a calm and relaxed manner and to us appears 'normal'. Moreover the boundaries of normal are extensive: thus some horses may have a peculiarity of gait or a certain stiffness which for them is normal.

The objective of this chapter is to help the horse owner recognise healthy signs so they are better able to distinguish any change from the norm in their horse, or any potential problem developing. What you are looking for are changes in temperament, the development of unusual stiffness, or an altered gait pattern.

For some of us it may be more difficult to know the normal responses of our horse because perhaps we have not owned him for very long; knowing what is normal and manageable, and therefore functioning correctly, is therefore harder to judge. Hopefully the guidelines given here will make you clearly aware of the 'normal' observations, and you will then be able to determine irregularity more readily.

In the Stable

The stable should have plenty of headroom, and be light and airy with good ventilation; if possible it should be in peaceful surroundings. Feeding off the floor is healthier for the horse: it is a more natural position with regard to his teeth balance and jaw alignment, and there is no risk of him getting dust in his eyes as he would with a hay rack, or of a leg becoming caught with a haynet. The floor should be well drained, and adequately covered with bedding right up to the door to prevent him slipping when he lies down or stands up; standing on a covered floor is also more comfortable for him, especially in the winter, and reduces jar to his legs and frame.

The doorway must be wide enough to allow the horse easy passage, and the lower door should not be so high that he must strain his neck to look out. Personally I am not a fan of toys or treats hanging down, as I believe they could have a deleterious effect on posture and teeth alignment.

NORMAL SIGNS OF HEALTHY HORSE	INTERPRETATION
Overall he looks healthy, happy and alert	There is nothing wrong with him: he is keen and ready for day ahead.
Eyes bright and nostrils clean. Regular, steady breathing pattern.	His respiratory system is in good order and he feels well in himself.
Stands square in box (stall) and has no difficulty in moving back from door when asked to do so.	No problems with posture and movement co-ordination.
His box (stall) is generally clean and no more disturbed than you would expect.	Internally he feels fine: no problems with colic or intestinal disorder.
His bedding is not over- or under-wet (daily condition of his bed is a guide to his water consumption: any change from normal may indicate a problem).	His kidneys are in good order: the electrolyte balance is good.
Able to eat food off floor and from bowl on floor.	His teeth function is good, no problems/pain in his back.
He doesn't mind having his rugs (blankets) put on and they stay where they should be and do not slip.	He is comfortable in himself and well balanced muscularly.
Happy to lift his limbs to have feet picked out.	His co-ordination, self-awareness and balance are good (normal).
Lies down and gets up again easily and has the occasional roll.	The functional mobility of his spine and pelvis is good (normal).
Walks in and out of his box (stall) quietly and sensibly.	Not upset by restricted areas, and in control of his own body position: nothing abnormal.

In the Field

Ensuring good turn-out facilities all the year round will help the horse to maintain his equilibrium both mentally and physically. However, good paddock maintenance is essential to reduce the risk of injury and disease, and to ensure grazing of adequate quality and an even terrain for him to move about on. This means picking up droppings regularly, and rolling and harrowing the surface when seasonally appropriate.

EVALUATION OF THE NORMAL HORSE

NORMAL HORSE IN THE FIELD	INTERPRETATION
Walks with head carriage of normal height in a keen manner.	Horse is feeling normally supple and mobile.
Able to move backwards easily when a gate is opened/shut.	The horse is co-ordinated and comfortable in body and limb.
Moves off evenly and fluently, mobility and co-ordination good.	No lameness or internal pain.
Lies down and rolls from side to side, and gets up easily	Normally athletic: he is not suffering from any .physical problems.
Mixes well socially with others.	Temperament is stable: no psychological problems.
Turn-out rug (blanket) stays on correctly.	Skeletal co-ordination and muscle symmetry are good, and gait is level (normal).
Does not pull his shoes off.	Moves well bio-mechanically: no physical/nervous problems that would cause abnormal motion.

POTENTIAL HAZARDS	EFFECTS
Plants such as ragwort, laurel, yew.	Poisonous to horses, and if eaten can cause death.
Untidy, loose fencing, particularly wire.	Can lead to entrapment, causing injury (cuts, tears, bruising, fractures, tissue damage).
Poached/damaged, rutted ground.	Causes concussion and uneven weight distribution which could lead to soft tissue and body injury.

Standing in Hand

It is often possible to recognise a potential problem in your horse simply from the way he is standing. However, to do so it is important first to appreciate what constitutes *his* normal conformation and stance.

Observe first of all how the horse stands when he is at rest, without attempting to make him stand square: this should give a clear idea as to his natural posture and outlook. Then stand him square and check his symmetry: it is essential to use a hard, level surface for this, and to spend as much time as is necessary to establish a good, four-square position. Always perform any exercise in hand on a hard, level surface: when walking or trotting the horse up this encourages better quality movement, and enables you to hear clearly the regularity – or not – of the horse's footfall.

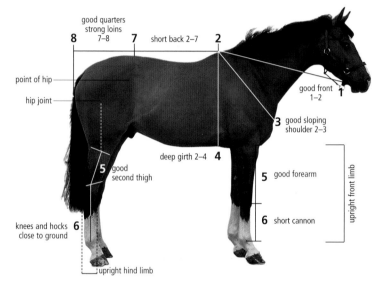

POINTS TO OBSERVE	INTERPRETATION
The angle of his head in relation to his neck.	Dictates flexibility of neck and carriage of head.
The angle of neck to shoulder.	Dictates how easily, or not, he can elevate his shoulder, and how much he can use his neck for balance.
The slope of his shoulder, and development of muscles that support forelimbs.	Dictates scope of shoulder movement.
The development of the muscle that covers shoulder blade and runs into back.	Dictates how easily he will carry saddle/driving harness.
The shape of his topline.	Dictates how well/badly he moves, how easily/difficult he will find suppling exercise.
Development of his hindquarters: how evenly his muscles are distributed.	Dictates the extent of his engagement and power.

14

FRONT VIEW

OBSERVATION	INTERPRETATION
How symmetrical is the horse's face?	Lack of symmetry – *eg* one droopy ear, one cheek bigger – may indicate pain/injury.
Posture: does horse stand square?	Lack of symmetry – *eg* one hip-bone higher, one point of shoulder higher/lower – may indicate pain/injury.
Muscle development of chest and underside of neck, should appear loose and even.	Uneven development may indicate pain/injury (not necessarily in chest or neck).
Do his limbs look level and his feet equally balanced?	Important for easy, stress-free movement.
Development of fore limb (upper) muscles.	Degree of development indicates how well – or not – horse is using his hindquarters to propel himself forwards: over-developed forelimb muscle might indicate pain in the hind limb(s) and/or back.

Check for symmetry either side of a straight line through centre of the knee, fetlock and foot

SIDE VIEW

OBSERVATION	INTERPRETATION
Positioning of hocks and hind limbs.	Good conformation means optimum propulsion and engagement.
Hang of tail: not clamped in, droopy, not too high.	Indicates degree of flexibility in the back.

REAR VIEW

OBSERVATION	INTERPRETATION
How evenly are the muscles developed?	Even development denotes correct use of muscles.
How even/level are the tubersacralae (jumper's bump)?	A level jumper's bump indicates good pelvic power and flexibility.
Tubercoxae level (point of hip).	Levelness indicates good pelvis and hind leg function.
Development of second thigh.	Good, even development optimises the power of the hind limbs to the quarters.

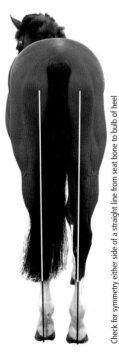

Check for symmetry either side of a straight line from seat bone to bulb of heel

15

Walking in Hand

EVALUATION OF THE NORMAL HORSE

Perform all movement on a suitable surface with plenty of room. Spend time listening and watching the overall impression. The handler should be positioned on the horse's left side at his shoulder, and must look ahead and move straight. Beware of potential hazards, and ensure that the horse can be controlled at all times. When he moves off he should do so with an active, energetic stride, and walk with his hind legs stepping well up underneath his body. The overall picture should be of symmetry and activity. Here is what to look for in the normal horse:

FRONT VIEW

OBSERVATION	INTERPRETATION
Note how each foot is placed to the ground; note the stride length.	A level stride and even footfall indicates an evenly balanced foot.
Good head and neck posture (1).	Satisfactory sensory and motor function.

REAR VIEW

OBSERVATION	INTERPRETATION
Observe the rise and fall of each hindquarter (2).	An even rise and fall indicates good mobility.
Movement of tail.	Held in midline and moving with relaxed, even swing indicates free-moving, healthy spine.
Note the swing and fluency of hind limbs; does the horse track up well (his hind foot should fall in to the track of the imprint of the front foot on each side)?	Good stride length and athletic movement indicates a healthy, supple horse: no problems.

SIDE VIEW

OBSERVATION	INTERPRETATION
Head on neck: should be soft, relaxed and mobile.	Fluid and easy movement.
Length of stride: should be even, with all four limbs appearing to match in fluidity and rhythm (3).	Good body control.
Look for pay-out and lengthening of muscle over shoulder onto trunk and through back.	Good muscle tone.
Should be some appearance of movement through the back itself.	Mobility.
Good bending of knee and hock joints with good length of stride.	Free flowing.

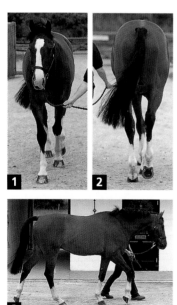

1

2

3

Trotting in Hand

The handler asks for trot and maintains his position by the horse's shoulder, asking him to go forwards from the hindquarters. Allow enough freedom of his head and neck, and perform a medium-paced trot. The horse should move with an active, level stride, and any unlevelness, stiffness or crookedness would indicate a problem. Viewed from in front and/or from behind, the horse should be straight *ie*, the forelegs and hind legs should be in line and not deviating to one side or the other. Here is what to look for:

FRONT VIEW

OBSERVATION	INTERPRETATION
Movement should be smooth and unrestricted, with level stride and equal footfall, and the head, neck and body should be relaxed **(4)**.	No problems. If the horse's head bobs up or down beyond the level of his normal head carriage, he is lame in his leg or foot.

REAR VIEW

OBSERVATION	INTERPRETATION
Movement should be active, engaged and forward, the hindquarters moving like two pistons evenly and smoothly **(5)**.	Mobile, supple muscular skeletal frame.
Limbs should be straight in movement, footfall should be even.	Activity and soundness are good: no problems.

SIDE VIEW

OBSERVATION	INTERPRETATION
Good rhythmical fluid appearance.	Horse is supple and mobile.
Stride length: should be equal **(6)**.	No problems in legs or feet.
Going forwards actively	Spinal and limb flexibility is good: no problems.

TROT TO WALK

OBSERVATION	INTERPRETATION
Does the horse maintain rhythm and balance?	If yes to all these: no problems. Any jerk, jar, unlevelness or stiffness would indicate pain or injury.
Do the hind legs step well under his body as he slows down?	Good control and engagement.
Do his hindquarters maintain engagement?	Flexible joints and spine.
Are the head and neck carried level, and without jerking up and down?	No uneven weight bearing.
Do the spinal muscles look relaxed and supple?	No counter balancing or compensation taking place.

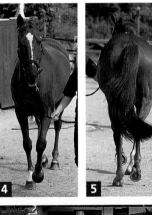

Turning on a 5m circle

'Turning short' is a good way to assess a horse's overall co-ordination and flexibility. However, as a useful comparative analysis the manner in which the horse turns must be consistent, *ie* he must be asked to perform the turn in the same way each time, and able to do so without change in his manner.

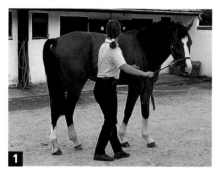

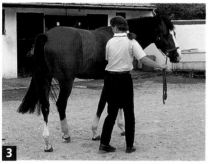

OBSERVATION	INTERPRETATION
Horse is able to bend head to side from top part of neck easily **(1)**.	Flexibility is good: no stiffness or restriction.
Movement continues through rest of neck smoothly and easily.	Flexibility of spine and in associated soft tissue is good.
The outside fore limb advances forwards with a good length of stride **(2)**.	No problem in ability of shoulder muscle to extend.
The horse moves forwards around you with good lateral bend through his body **(3)**.	Good flexibility.
The hind legs cross well over **(3)**, the outside leg actively flexes and is carried smoothly away from his body as he moves forwards and round; weight is transferred across pelvic area without sign of discomfort **(4)**.	No problems in pelvic area or in hind limbs.
Horse can perform several circles without hesitation or change in his manner.	Horse is perfectly supple throughout his body.

Rein Back

Generally the horse will step backwards with no problem when opening a gate out hacking, and when you ask him to move away from the stable door as you go in or out. As an observation exercise, it is a useful test to assess his co-ordination, and how easily he moves. It is important when you ask the horse to step back to do so by putting a hand against his chest,

TIP: An extra dimension to this test is to perform it on a slight uphill incline. This tests his flexibility to an even greater degree.

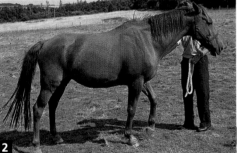

and not to restrain his head or pull on his halter/bridle in any way; and once he has stepped backwards two to four steps, bring him forwards a few strides.

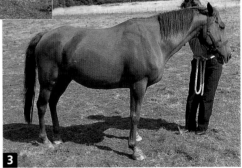

OBSERVATION	INTERPRETATION
Head and neck remain relaxed and at shoulder height **(1)**.	No pain or stiffness in neck.
Fore limbs take even strides, clearing the ground well.	Flexibility and co-ordination in lower neck and shoulder is good.
Back remains level and soft throughout the exercise **(2)** and keeps straight.	Spinal mobility is good.
Hind legs engage and take level, regular steps backwards **(3)**.	Range of motion in the stifle and back is good.

Palpating the Normal Horse

Palpation is the technique used in any initial examination of a horse, to assess his normal physical state, and with a view to detecting areas where a problem might develop; it can also be used as a means to relax him.

The first step in learning how to palpate your horse and to gain his and your confidence is to start grooming him using your hands – even if he is very sensitive and tickly. Try out different levels of hand contact, too – surprisingly, a sensitive horse will often appreciate a greater degree of pressure. The following scale, numbered out of 10, is to help you gauge the amount of pressure you might need to apply: light: 1–3/10; medium: 4–6/10; heavy: 7–10/10.

When palpating your horse, if you know he is worried about any one particular area then leave that spot until the end when he will be more relaxed. And if you find he reacts by moving away from what you are doing, try quietly resting your hands over the area and allowing them just to warm and relax the tissues. Also, breathing in a gentle and deep way yourself can help reassure him. This technique can also have an extremely beneficial effect on a fatigued or stressed horse.

PALPATING HAND EXERCISES FOR YOURSELF

Before you start any palpation or massage session, it is important to warm up your own muscles. This will help to diminish the risk of strains, as well as to maximise the stretch of your hands.

Exercise 1
To increase hand span
- Stretch your hands wide open **(1)**.
- Use a surface to 'walk' your stretched open hand along.
- Open wide and hold the stretch for 5–10 seconds.

Exercise 2 *Wrist extension*
- Place fingers against a wall, and drop wrist down **(2)**.
- Feel the stretch through hand into wrist.
- Hold slowly to count of 10, and release.
- Do both hands.

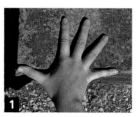

Exercise 3
To strengthen hands
- Use hand grips to develop hand strength.
- Build up your strength by gradually increasing resistance

PREPARATION FOR PALPATION

Before each session, make sure you are well prepared: this checklist will help.
- Tub of saddle soap/piece of chalk, to mark any problem areas.
- A headcollar (halter) large enough to move back over the upper neck.
- A lead rope, not a chain.

- If working on your own, secure the horse by tying him loosely to bailer twine.
- If a handler is present, have them on the same side as yourself throughout the session. Discourage them from actively touching the horse during the palpatory examination. Advise them to hold the rope, not the headcollar (halter), with hands quietly by their sides.
- Don't let the horse eat; do not stand him by the door or under low beams.
- Make sure the atmosphere is relaxed and peaceful.

Palpation

Palpation techniques are used to detect tone, pain and resistance in the tissues. Varying amounts of pressure may be used, from light, to moderate, to heavy.

METHOD OF PALPATION

Always use the pads of your fingers and thumbs and/or the flat of your hand. It is usual to do one side of the horse all the way through from head to tail, and then repeat on the other side. However, if you are not sure of what constitutes normal, and whilst you are learning, do one side of the neck, say, and then the other side as a comparison, and so on for the rest of body. Eventually, for fluidity and full appreciation, do all of one side and then move to the other. You may find it easier to detect heat changes or differences using your hand placed over the area.

TIP: Long finger nails sometimes make palpation more difficult, so although it is not impossible to do a good job, they are best kept reasonably short.

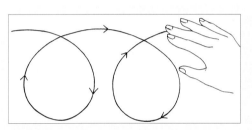

Circles

These are normally performed over the spinal muscles. Using one or more finger(s), work over tissue in a rotating movement to detect resistance and spasms.

Zigzags

Normally used to identify soft tissue resistance in the wither and hindquarter areas. Move fingers in a zigzag direction through tissues.

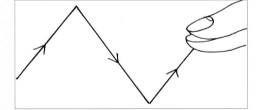

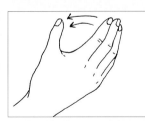

Cupped hand (cat's paw)

Used around the chest and stomach area, also on the hindquarters for the hamstrings. Using a soft cupped hand, move across tissue to detect skin resistance. Start with light to moderate pressure.

Line palpation

Can be used anywhere, but most often in the shoulder and chest area. Move the finger(s) or hand across or through tissue in a stroking motion to detect abnormalities such as tone, pain and resistance. Use varying amounts of pressure from light, to moderate, to heavy.

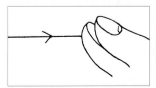

Palpating Techniques

Palpation is the art of touch using your fingers and hands to feel the tissues. Be sensitive: too little pressure will irritate your horse and he will react by twitching as if you are a fly. The opposite is to be too heavy and cause a pain reaction. Instead of using brushes to groom your horse, substitute this palpatory routine with your hand, and horses that are sensitive skinned will relax and learn to enjoy being touched. You don't have to perform a full palpatory examination every day (see page 47).If you are following on with a massage routine, then use saddle soap to mark areas of adverse tissue change. As you palpate, keep observing the posture of his head and neck, the expression in his eye, and his breathing rate, and you will see if he is happy or in discomfort.

TIP: If the horse suddenly reacts and appears uncomfortable, then re-check the area using a slightly different grade of pressure; compare it with the other side, and re-check. If you keep getting the same response then this could be a potential problem area.

PALPATION	INTERPRETATION
Rest hands and fingers on skin surface.	Feel the liveliness of the tissue.
Relax and breathe out.	Observe his response.
Lower your body posture and head and gently lean into your hands.	Feel the tissue change and become loose.
Register the texture of the skin.	Where there is tissue damage there will be scarring of tissue; this feels hard and knotted. Could be caused by friction from saddle or saddle pads or direct muscle damage.
Feel the tone of the tissue.	Muscle tone that is weak will feel floppy and loose; if it is tense it will feel rigid and taut.
Identify temperature.	**Heat**: indicates inflamed tissue. Normal: warmth as in normal healthy tissue. **Cold**: indicates poor blood supply.
Gauge the horse's sensitivity.	If the horse is irritable and twitchy, it is because he is sore and reactive. No reaction – dull, lifeless – horse may simply be insensitive, *but* also he may be ill.
Observe and listen.	**Eyes**: wide open and 'starey': indicates worry or fear. Closing and 'dewy'-looking: indicates calm and sedation effect. **Breathing**: rapid and obvious: can indicate stress. Deep and quiet: associated with relaxation, comfort.

Palpating Techniques

The supporting structures, such as ligaments and tendons, should be checked daily both before and after exercise in order to identify any early warning signs of strain or injury. If there are any signs of heat or swelling, rest the horse and call your vet to discuss the situation. Every horse's leg is slightly different and may have old lumps and bumps of no significance; however, early detection of a genuine potential problem is vital if further damage by continuing a high level of exercise is to be avoided. Use the following numbered routine to check the horse's leg thoroughly:

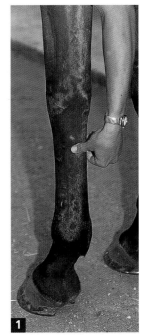

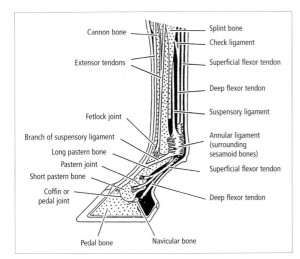

Cannon bone — Splint bone
Check ligament
Extensor tendons — Superficial flexor tendon
Deep flexor tendon
Suspensory ligament
Fetlock joint
Branch of suspensory ligament — Annular ligament (surrounding sesamoid bones)
Long pastern bone
Pastern joint — Superficial flexor tendon
Short pastern bone
Coffin or pedal joint — Deep flexor tendon
Pedal bone   Navicular bone

1 Palpate with the hand over the hoof wall for heat or direct muscle damage.
2 Feel for the digital pulse on the inside and outside of the back of the pastern; if there is any problem, the pulse will pound very distinctly.
3 Slide a hand down the front of leg, the thumb feeling the grooves between the cannon bone and the splint bones. Identify thickenings/heat/swelling.
4 Thumb and finger palpate superficial and deep flexor tendons and suspensory ligaments **(1)**: these should be cool, with no swelling.
5 Raise the horse's leg and palpate the soft tissues in more detail **(2)**: the superficial flexor, the deep flexor tendon and the suspensory ligament.

Head and Neck

Some horses may be over-reactive due to ear problems or nervousness, so take plenty of time to relax your horse. The head and neck area can be sore because of direct injury or excessive pressure. If the horse has teeth problems it can cause soreness around the jaw and ears. Also when working incorrectly the neck area can become affected.

Do not pull down on the horse's headcollar (halter), but lift it slightly so as to relax any pressure it might exert over the poll. Work from the near side first, then repeat on the other side.

ZONE 1: FRONT FACE, POLL AND BETWEEN EARS
Front face
What you feel: Should feel flat and relaxed.

- Stand on the near side with the right hand holding the cheekpiece of the headcollar (halter).
- Lay the left hand flat on his forehead **(1)**. Rest for a few seconds, then move slowly at a light 3/10 pressure down the front of his face to nose **(2)**.

Poll and between ears
What you feel: Feels soft and without reaction or impression of swelling.

- Replace hand slowly at forehead and move up and over top of skull between ears – feel around base of ears **(3)**.
- Using your thumb, move from poll down over area behind ears to top of jaw **(4)**.
- Use a light pressure x 3.
- Repeat upwards and downwards.
- Then repeat using a medium pressure x 3.

ZONE 2: SIDE OF FACE AND UNDER JAW

What you feel: Feels loose and soft.

- Using left hand, move from ear down side of face to muzzle. Use light pressure **(5)**.
- Place right hand underneath jaw and move from throat to muzzle **(6)**.

ZONE 3: TOP AND SIDE OF NECK

What you feel: Feels toned, but even contours all through.

- Left hand now rests on side of face or headcollar (halter), or on neck. Right hand strokes at medium pressure from top of neck nearest skull down top part of neck where it joins to wither **(7)**.
- Repeat x 3.

ZONE 4: SIDE AND UNDER-SURFACE OF NECK

What you feel: Tissue under neck feels loose and mobile.

- The neck vertebrae will feel hard, but tissue will feel unreactive.
- From top of neck by jaw to shoulder blade.
- Use left hand light pressure x 3, and then medium pressure x 3 to stroke tissue. If sensitive remember this is a bony area and back off slightly.
- Then feel under-surface of neck. Right hand rests at base of neck **(8)**.

Forelimbs and Shoulders

The area can be sensitive, so be quiet and firm around the shoulder muscles. This soreness may arise because the feet are sore, causing an altered way of moving, or fatigue from over-exertion. Horses also become tight in this area from problems in the tissues higher up over the withers and back.

Work on the left side, then repeat on the other side.

ZONE 1: BASE OF NECK BETWEEN SHOULDER AND NECK

What you feel: Should feel soft and relaxed.

- With right hand resting on shoulder, left hand strokes down from wither in front of shoulder blade into neck area **(1)**.
- Do light pressure 2–3/10 x 3.
- Then repeat at medium 4–6/10 x 3.

ZONE 2: SHOULDER MUSCLES

What you feel: Feels soft and filled.

- Left hand rests firmly on shoulder.
- Using right hand, stroke at light pressure x 3 from top of scapula down to top of leg. Do in three divisions **(2)**.
- Then do them at medium pressure x 3 each division.

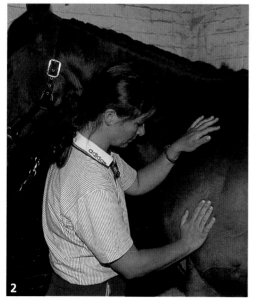

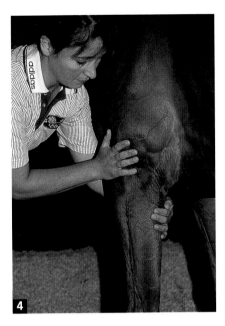

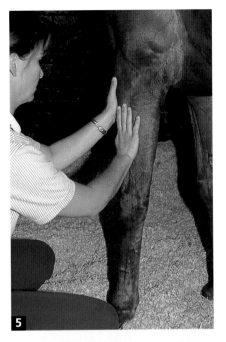

ZONE 3: FRONT AND UNDER-SURFACE OF CHEST

What you feel: Consistent contour, evenly defined.

- Use left hand, with fingers facing inwards to where the girth goes, with rest of hand flat on chest muscles **(3, left)**.
- Draw hand towards throat, using light pressure x 3, then medium pressure x 3. You will feel sternum or chest bone in the middle.

ZONE 4: TOP HALF OF FORELEG

What you feel: Firm, well toned feel. Skin on inside of upper leg feels slightly loose.

- Using left hand, palpate light pressure inside forelimb round to front of upper leg **(4)**.
- Then switch hands: using right hand, stroke lengthways in two sections down outside of limb to knee level **(5)**.
- Repeat x 3.
- Then using right hand, palpate using stroking technique from elbow to back of knee **(6)**.
- Repeat x 3 light pressure.
- Repeat using medium pressure x 3 all areas.

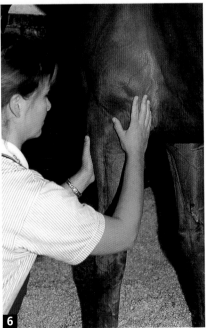

Withers and Back

This area is where the tack rests and can have friction marks and areas of inflammation from excessive pressure. Palpation of this area after exercise is a good way of monitoring and detecting these changes.

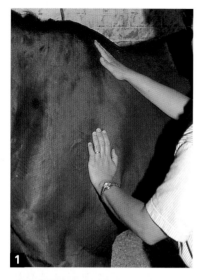

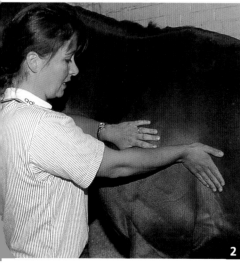

ZONE 1: SHOULDER BLADE AND CHEST WALL
From top of scapula and down side of chest to girth area

What you feel: Feels soft and undulating, then increasingly less depth of tissue down over the chest.
- Left hand resting on shoulder.
- Using just finger pads of right hand, sweep over scapula, then apply whole hand contact down side of chest wall **(1)**.
- Turn fingers downwards halfway down, to continue in one sweeping motion **(2)**.
- Repeat x 3, using light pressure.
- Using medium pressure, stroke x 3.

ZONE 2: WITHERS
What you feel: Feels bony: less depth of tissue over this area. Should be smooth.
- Over withers from neck into back **(3)**.
- Using right hand, stroke at a light pressure.
- Repeat x 3.
- Using medium pressure, stroke x 3.

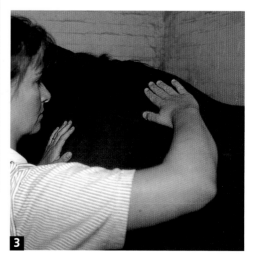

28

ZONE 3: THE BACK TOPLINE AREA

What you feel: Will be unreactive and of even texture; good muscle quality.

- Work from withers through to end of back **(4)**.
- Using a flat hand (right), stroke along the back.
- You may need to do this in two divisions.

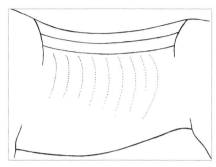

The divisions of the back

- Do x 3 light pressure, and then medium pressure x 3.
- Repeat, drawing circles along the tissue of back (see page 21) **(5)**.
- Do x 1 light pressure, then repeat x 1 at medium pressure.

ZONE 4: RIB ANGLES AND ABDOMEN

The horse can be sensitive in the area, so watch he does not kick up or bite.

Rib angles

What you feel: Unreactive but taut texture.

- Using middle three fingers of right hand, draw lines from top, down between bony projections (these are ribs) on the horse's side **(6)**.
- Do x 3 at several points using light pressure, then repeat at medium.

Abdomen

What you feel: Relaxed, well toned feel; should not be tucked up or dropped.

- Using flat of either hand, stroke firmly along middle from behind forelimbs to approximately two-thirds of the way back on abdomen **(7)**.
- May need to divide up to encompass whole area.
- Do x 3 each division at light pressure, followed by medium pressure x 3.

Hindquarters

This is a large area of muscle mass, responsible for supplying the power of movement. Don't be too timid in your palpation, but really feel and appreciate its size.

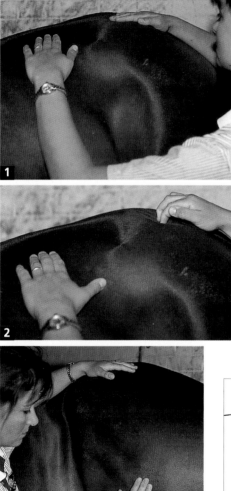

ZONE 1: GLUTEI – TOP OF BUTTOCKS

What you feel: Good even texture, with a good springy tone.

- Using right hand, stroke over the low back into top of buttock alongside jumper's bump (sacroiliac joint) **(1)**.
- Do x 3 light pressure and x 3 medium pressure.
- Repeat using zigzag technique at x 1 light and x 1 medium pressure (see page 21) **(2)**.

ZONE 2: BICEPS FEMORIS MUSCLE – MIDDLE OF QUARTER

What you feel: Firm, taut feel.

- From jumper's bump, sweep down middle of quarter to stifle (don't touch area of stifle) in stroking action **(3)**.
- Divide into sections to encompass whole area (see diagram below).
- Do x 3 light pressure then x 3 medium pressure each division.

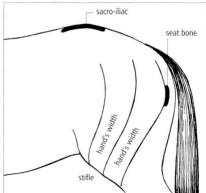

The divisions of the hindquarters

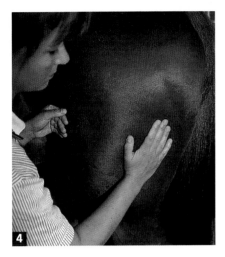

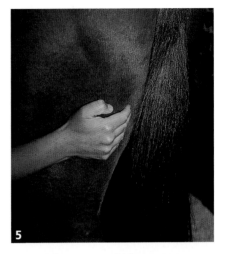

ZONE 3: SEMI-TENDINOSUS – FAR SIDE OF QUARTER

What you feel: Outside: soft and malleable; hindquarter: firm but mobile.

Can be sensitive here, so stand well to side. If horse is reactive, work from opposite side *ie* to palpate near side, go to off side.

- Work from back of quarter at start of tail, down side and back of bottom **(4)**.
- Use 'cat's paw' for palpation technique down outside **(5)**.
- Do light x 3 and medium x 3.
- Use flat hand stroking palpation technique over quarter area.
- Do light x 3 and medium x 3.

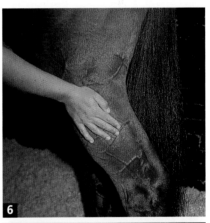

ZONE 4: EXTENSOR DIGITORUM LATERALIS AND GASTROCNEMIUS – SECOND THIGH

Stroke area from second thigh towards top of hock on outside area. Do x 3 at light pressure **(6)**.

- Repeat x 3 at medium pressure.
- Stroke top inside and back of second thigh towards hock **(7)**.
- Do x 3 at light pressure.
- Repeat x 3 at medium pressure.

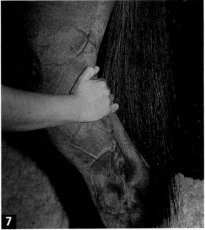

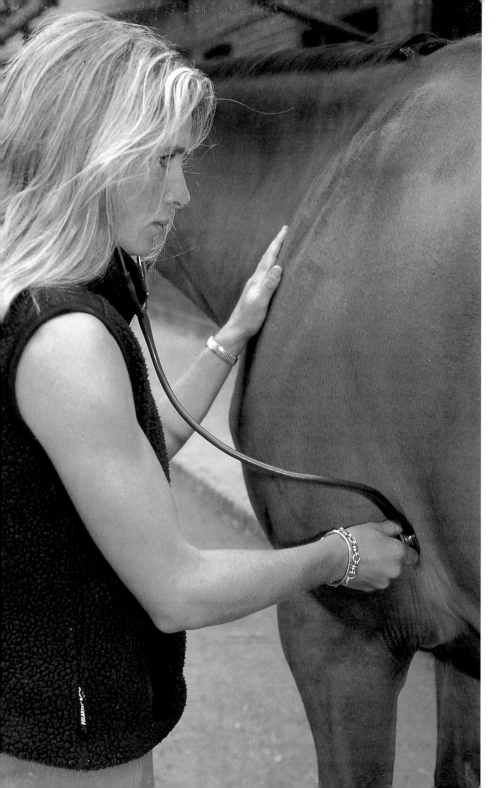

A badly fitted rug (blanket) that is too wide around the chest will impede mobility. Lack of padding under the roller will cause pressure points across the spine. Rollers/surcingles: most rugs are now designed with crossover straps, doing away with the need for rollers. However, if you do need to use a roller or surcingle, make sure that as the horse puts his head up and down there is no pressure over his spine.

Identifying Problems

In order to prevent a problem occurring you have to minimise the risks, and you should also be able to recognise subtle changes that could indicate that the horse is feeling pain or discomfort somewhere. Horses can't talk and tell us what's wrong, and many are very stoical in that they will carry on for a long time whilst experiencing pain, indeed to the extent that they may develop compensatory problems and altered movement patterns. By the time their trouble is obvious it is very likely of long standing and, together with the associated problems it has caused, fairly serious. Critical evaluation of any changes in the horse's behaviour and movement should help to pre-empt this process of decline.

Use the following checklist as a guide in assessing your horse's state of wellbeing:
- Take the horse's temperature. • Check his respiratory rate.
- Monitor his fluid intake. • Discuss all pain-related symptoms and signs with your veterinary surgeon. • Check that the horse is being exercised/turned out regularly.

Equally important to his welfare is the way he is looked after, and as well as the quality of his feed, you might check the following:
- His rugs (blankets) should fit correctly. • An adequate layer of bedding should cover the stable floor. • His hay and food are best given at floor level.• Be sure that the doorways are wide enough.

Stable Behaviour

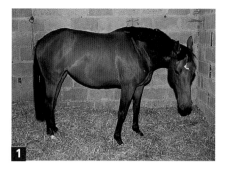

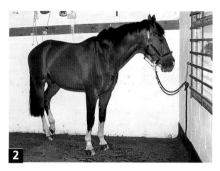

OBSERVATIONS	INTERPRETATION
Dull in the eye/coat lifeless **(1)**.	Horse is off colour: check temperature and speak to vet. Monitor closely.
Having difficulties eating.	Examine mouth. Have teeth checked. Feed hay and concentrates on the floor to ensure correct teeth alignment.
Change in drinking pattern: too little or too much. Check condition of bedding, colour and smell of urine.	Any change might indicate blood disorder, internal problems. Discuss with vet.
Mobility around box (stall): Not able to move across. Not able to get up easily. Problems lying down. Injuring limbs.	Painful somewhere, perhaps pelvis or feet. Back/limb problems. Not co-ordinating well.
Bruising of chest wall muscles.	Horse is lying on his front feet. Place protective donut boots on fetlocks.
Rugs: He tears them off. Becomes aggressive when they are put on or taken off.	Check spine and soft tissues for irritation. Check fit of rugs (blankets) for adverse pressure/impingement. Place padding over withers. Shorten collar of rug (blanket).
Altered posture **(2)**: Standing resting against surface. Pointing toe in front. Standing in stretched out position. Standing tucked up.	Taking weight off pelvis and back limbs, indicating pain/discomfort. Pain in foot. Pain in back. Pain somewhere, possibly internal.
Resentful of routine picking out of feet. Rubbing legs against object. Biting himself.	Problems of balance; pain in back, shoulder, pelvis. Foot or pelvic pain, or inflammation. Stress
On tacking up in box (stall)/seeing saddle, horse runs to back of box (stall).	Not happy in ridden exercise, possibly because of pain caused by ill-fitting saddle, or back pain.
Rushes through doorways.	Fear of catching hips on door frame.

Standing Square

Choose a flat, even surface to examine your horse, and start by observing his natural stance, not 'standing him up square' until you have done so.

FRONT VIEW

OBSERVATIONS	INTERPRETATION
Head and Neck	
Held tilted.	Discomfort in mouth; head (ear); neck; back.
Too high.	Pain in foot (feet); wither area; back.
Twisted.	General disability; could be internal pain.
Too low.	Generally unwell; musculoskeletal problem.
Muscles more developed one side than other.	Overworking one side, or underworking the other.
One nostril drooped and crooked.	Facial palsy – neurological. *See vet.*
Hang of chest muscles	
Sucked in.	Muscles torn or damaged.
Hole on one side of chest.	
Forelimbs	
Horse standing with forelegs abnormally far apart/close together.	Horse has changed its posture to alleviate discomfort. Could be caused by foot imbalance or pain in foot; or pain/discomfort in back.
Standing with one foreleg in front of other.	
Feet	
Toes too long.	Horse not being shod regularly enough/correctly.
Incorrect medial/lateral balance of foot.	
Horn of foot crumbling/damaged.	Nutrition problems; seek advice.

SIDE VIEW

Work on both sides: start from the nose and work up to the eyes and then to the ears; observe the head-on-neck position.

OBSERVATIONS	INTERPRETATION
Nose poking out.	Neck problems.
Muscles on under-side of **neck** are solid.	
Forearm over-developed.	Not using back end correctly – horse pulling itself along with its forehand. Indicates back/hindleg/pelvic/saddle problems.
Absence of muscle development in **shoulders**, shortening of stride.	Foot/back/saddle/leg problems.
Hard and soft swellings in **withers** area.	Saddle/rug (blanket)/rolling contusions.
Abnormal contour of top of withers.	
Too much muscle development behind **scapulae**.	Not working through shoulder correctly.
Hollows behind scapulae.	Saddle pain.
	Forelimb lameness.
	Damage to muscles.
Loss of muscle through **back** area where saddle would sit.	Back condition *ie* inflammation/saddle problems/lack of correct exercise.
White hair marks (see page 46).	Saddle/harness impingement.
Top of spine swollen and thickened.	

OBSERVATIONS	INTERPRETATION
Over-developed **buttock** muscles (superficial glutei).	Low back pain.
Under-developed buttock **(1)**.	Limb/pelvic pain, or incorrect exercise.
Prominent tubersacralae (jumper's bump)	Conformation/loss of muscle/damage to sacroiliac.
Over-prominent **seat bones**.	Loss of muscle: may be from not working correctly.
Loss of muscle tone around **stifle** (biceps femoris/ vastus lateralis).	Limb pain; strain from incorrect work.
Swellings inside and outside **hock**.	Joint pain.
Thickening inside below hock.	Strain to ligament.
Enlarged joints.	Generally caused by concussion. Could lead to lameness.
Foot looks unbalanced: from side, look at pastern–foot axis, and pay attention to whether heels are collapsed or contracted, and length of toe **(2)**.	Problem may be metabolic/nutritional. Toe too long and collapsed heels are often caused by irregular or poor shoeing.

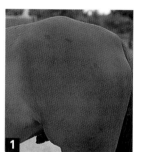

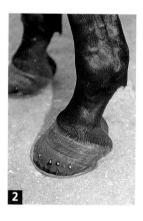

REAR VIEW

Stand on a raised surface so you can look down onto the horse's back: like this you can best evaluate the muscle balance of the horse's two sides, and the straightness of his spine **(3)**. Other anatomical variations in the skeleton may also be more obvious from higher up.

Next, encourage the horse to lower his head: as he does so, look along the topline of his crest and observe the muscle definition; again, it is easier to assess any abnormalities/unequal muscle development from a raised position. Check the symmetry of the withers, too – one side may be further forwards or higher, indicating possible strain or injury, or bad foot balance.

In standing a distance away behind the horse, any problems regarding muscle wastage/development, or soft tissue/skeletal symmetry, can be seen much more clearly. These might include the following: asymmetry of the sacroiliac joint (jumper's bump), or of the tuber coxis (pinbones), or of the seat bones **(4)**; and/or weak and wasted inside thigh muscles.

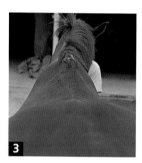

sacroiliac joint

tuber coxis

seat bones

Abnormal Movement

We rarely see our horses moving freely as we are on top of them or behind them, or a rider is riding them for us. If you watch your horse move in hand as a veterinarian does, on a routine basis, you can assess and familiarise yourself with your horse's movement. Always remember to listen and watch and to spend plenty of time getting your eye in. Observe him from behind (1), in front (2), and each side

TIP: The handler must stay by the horse's shoulder to keep him straight, and should not look at him but should look ahead.

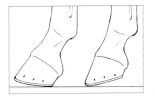

Left: Normal placement: heel first then toe
Right: Abnormal placement: toe to heel indicating heel pain

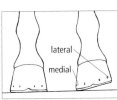

Left: Normal foot balance.
Right: Medial-lateral foot imbalance so that outside or inside edge lands first

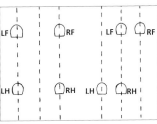

Left: Normal movement on two tracks.
Right: Abnormal movement on three tracks with quarters to the left

OBSERVATION	INTERPRETATION
Carrying head and neck in a stilted and restricted way.	Fore-limb pain could be bilateral. Neck problems. Stiffness/lameness.
Uneven footfall.	Lame.
Uneven placement of foot to ground **(above left)**.	Foot balance/foot pain such as corn or navicular.
Abnormal swing of leg ie dishing.	Lame in limb, or back problem, or conformation.
Moving in an unco-ordinated way.	Spinal/limb pain or neurological problem.
Moving very wide behind.	Musculo-skeletal lameness; spinal pain.
Loss of propulsion and piston action of hindquarters.	Muscles of limb/hindquarter unequally developed. Loss of spinal mobility. Lame.
Carrying quarters to one side, moving on three tracks instead of two **(above right).**	As above.
Tail carried rigidly, or too much to one side.	Musculo-skeletal problem.
On placement of hind limb, deviation or twist through the leg.	Lameness or muscle weakness.

TRANSITION FROM WALK TO TROT

OBSERVATION	INTERPRETATION
On transition lurches forwards.	Loss of normal movement: lame, or muscle weakness.
Unable to swing fore limb through fully, and so appears to hover in air.	Lame in neck, shoulder, forelimb.
Back legs do not step under body, but appear to trail.	Feels pain in back/quarters/hindlegs: musculo-skeletal dysfunction – check for lameness.
Inconsistent head position: head may persistently tilt one way.	Pain in neck or feet.
Note: If in doubt, repeat several times.	

AT TROT

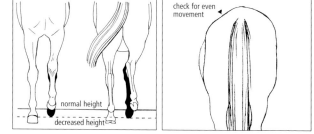

- Listen for regularity of footfalls. If uneven, horse is lame.
- Observe from behind, from in front, and from each side at a good distance away: notice whether the movement gets worse, or stays the same.
- If lame, the horse usually nods his head. If lame in front his head drops as his sound leg meets the ground, and rises when the painful leg makes contact.
- Short pottering strides in front: he is lame in both front legs.
- Hind leg lameness: horse lowers his head as the sore leg meets the ground.
- Watch out for any sign of decreased flexion of the hind limbs, causing the toe to drag (**above left** – area in black indicates the decreased height of the lame foot/limb).

- As he moves away from you, study the rise and fall of the quarters: they should move evenly, and with no deviation in movement to either side (**above right**).

TRANSITION FROM TROT TO WALK

- Observe the fluency and co-ordination of the horse's movement: if there is a problem he will look disjointed, and his back end will be slow to step under his body **(3)**.
- He will throw up his head **(4)**.
- His back legs will look as if they are trailing out behind him.

38

Turning Tight Circles

A horse finds it difficult to turn his body in a tight radius, and he will be easier to manoeuvre, and will move to best advantage, if the lead rope is attached to the outside of the headcollar **(1)**. The handler then guides him forwards and round in small circles.

- Repeat on both reins.

ADVERSE REACTIONS TO TURNING SHORT

- Sticks nose out **(2)**.
- Inability to turn head or neck to side so head tilts, or swings round like an ironing board **(3)**.
- No bend through neck as continues round **(4)**.
- Can't pivot on fore limbs **(5)**.
- 'Hobbles' round as if feet painful.
- Rushes backwards.
- Back shows no spinal curve as he turns, but is held rigid: his way of protecting painful back muscles.
- Unable to cross back legs past midline.
- Stilted action of outside hind leg **(6)**.
- Unhappy bearing weight on inside leg and hops round.

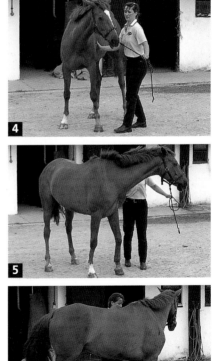

39

The Rein-Back

The rein-back is a test of co-ordination and flexibility. Ask the horse to step backwards by placing a hand against his chest **(1)**; and once he has completed as many steps as you ask, always make him walk forwards for the same number of steps – this will help his muscles relax and leave him more comfortable. A greater test is to ask him to rein back on a slight upward gradient: if he has a problem in his neck, back, pelvis or hindquarters he may find this difficult, or will be unable to perform the movement.

If the horse finds this exercise difficult or painful, he will react unfavourably; thus he might:

- drag the front feet
- go crookedly **(2)**
- be unhappy to bear weight behind
- throw up his head
- become rigid behind the saddle – his muscles will go into spasm **(3)**
- lock one or both stifles.

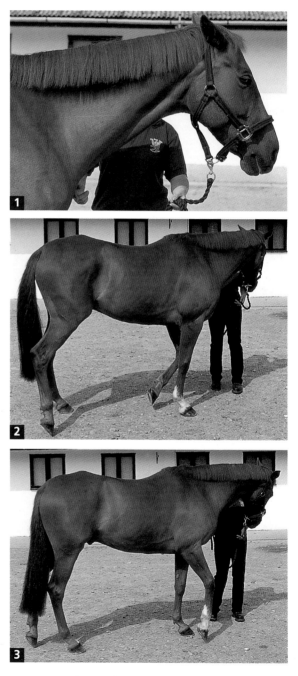

40

Ridden Exercise

SIGNS AND SYMPTOMS OF ABNORMAL
MOVEMENT AND/OR FUNCTION

When a horse fails to accomplish a movement we ask of him, there are several factors that should be considered when trying to establish why. It may be simply because of our own inadequate riding skills, or because we are still learning and do not yet have those skills! More worrying is a sudden or progressive change in the horse from being able to accomplish a movement easily and comfortably, and then not being able to do so. In a horse you know well it may be easy to know why; more difficult is to identify a potential area of unidentified pain in a horse you do not know, and in this instance you will have to rely on your own ability and those around you to detect it.

Never ignore your gut feeling and instinct – you don't have to comply if you feel you are being told to ignore something that you know is not right. Remember that your instructor, farrier, physiotherapist and vet should work as a team to help eliminate causative factors, and to advise and inform you of correct management.

TACKING UP

Note how the horse behaves when you tack him up: an aggressive or fearful reaction is a definite indication of discomfort. Look for the following to indicate potential problems:

- Horse resents tack, bites and kicks, groans **(1)**.
- Tack does not sit true, keeps moving.
- You can't ride level.

OBSERVATION	INTERPRETATION
When rider mounts	
Resents rider's weight being put in stirrup.	Saddle is pressing uncomfortably at stirrup bars/tree points.
Back is obviously sensitive when rider sits in saddle: horse may sink his back down or arch it violently.	Back is inflamed.
Bucks and kicks out.	Horse is uncomfortable, may be the saddle, or some other unidentified problem.
When first moves from stand to walk	
Very uncomfortable, sticks head in air. Runs off. Swishes tail a lot. Eye looks wild, fearful. General change in demeanour and expression.	Pain in the back, and/or girth area.

OBSERVATION	INTERPRETATION
Ridden problems	
Changes stride over rough or undulating ground.	Pain in foot and/or back.
Stumbles and trips.	
Goes crooked, or shortens stride going downhill.	
Stride generally becomes shorter.	
Fatigues quickly.	Pain or metabolic problem.
Sweats all over or excessively on one area **(2)**.	
Reluctant to go forwards on one rein.	Lameness/spinal stiffness.
Unable to bend on one rein.	Lame/musculo-skeletal weakness.
Has difficulty performing transitions:	
• back legs appear to trail	
• can't engage	
• falls onto forehand	
• bucks going into transitions	
• unable to maintain straightness	
Tilts head, or moves it excessively.	Feet/neck/back/mouth pain/bit/tack.
Unable to maintain correct diagonal or canter lead on one rein.	Limb, musculo-skeletal pain.

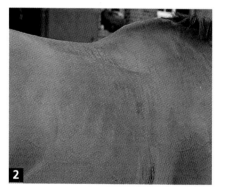

LATERAL MOVEMENT
In this type of work, the horse moves forwards and sideways simultaneously, to a greater or lesser degree. He must be well balanced and going forwards without resistance, and be able to maintain rhythm. For most lateral work he needs to be collected. The exceptions are leg yielding and turns on the forehand.

OBSERVATION	INTERPRETATION
Unable to go forwards and sideways **(3)**.	Horse is lame, or experiencing musculo-skeletal discomfort.
Loses power; no impulsion or rhythm; very tense; feels awkward, stiff; resents movement.	Check teeth, tack, or rider error.

JUMPING

Horses are trained to jump freely and with a rider, but there are many reasons why it may go wrong. A physical problem can also appear as a training problem, so respect advice from your trainer and veterinarian to distinguish between them.

If there is a problem when the horse is being ridden, examine him without the rider on to see if he still has difficulty. It may be worthwhile trying a change of rider, to see how someone else copes with the problem: a stronger rider may be better able to hold the horse together, and be more authoritative, whilst still being able to give feedback on their impression of the severity or relevance of the difficulties experienced. Alternatively, some horses may be better performing at lower levels of competition, with lesser demands placed upon them: a stronger, more ambitious rider might ask too much and overface the horse, compromising what ability he has.

SIGNS	INTERPRETATION
Can't make the height.	Rider is asking too much of horse.
Unable to do bounce fences.	Unable to do it physically.
Runs out to same side.	Pain: could be in foot/back/leg/mouth.
Always jumps to one side as	Reduced power due to
pushes off.	musculo-skeletal problem.
Always lands on same leg and won't change.	Discomfort or pain (as above).
Bucks and rushes off on landing **(4)**.	

Shoe Wear

The farrier (1) often gets a poor deal. In the worst instance he has to shoe wet and muddy feet, often with no one to hold the horse or lead it in and out of the stables; and no one communicates with him except to suggest he charges too much, or to let him know the horse is now lame and it is all his fault! So for a start, improve your relationship with your farrier. Ask if there is anything you can do to help with the nutrition of the horse's feet, what they were like to shoe.

Evidence of potential problems can start to show up very early on in the way the shoe wears. Look for the following:

- Excessive wear on one shoe.
- Unevenly distributed wear.
- Untoward stiffness or heaviness in the movement of limbs when horse is being shod.
- Thin soles.
- Collapsed heels.
- Contracted heels (2).
- Crumbling hoof wall.
- Changing foot/pastern axis.
- Losing shoes easily.
- Loss of medial/lateral (ie inside and outside) foot balance.

Tack

Poor performance and deterioration in muscle tone may be directly caused by badly fitting tack. With a properly fitting saddle and bridle the horse can move freely, without any pain or discomfort, and so has a better chance of performing to his best ability. Furthermore a correctly fitted saddle allows the rider to be balanced and centred on the horse, again optimising the chances of producing a good performance. However, the problems that can be caused by badly fitting tack are legion, and can have disastrous consequences of long standing **(4)**. The following chapter will deal with these problems in detail, and how to prevent them: this section is to identify problems which will lead to damage, or which may have caused it already.

Check your saddle regularly for damage or wear and tear: if it has a twisted tree from being driven over, or is damaged in some way, it will cause damage to your horse's back. Always have it checked if you think it has been subjected to abuse. Driving harness must also

1

IDENTIFYING PROBLEMS

OBSERVATION	INTERPRETATION
Take note of sweat marks.	Large areas of excessive sweating can be pain-related. Check symmetry of sweating to determine problem.
Look for soft swellings.	Saddle pressure or circulatory restriction can cause these lumps. Look to see if they are still there after a couple of hours **(1)**.
Look at lie of hair for friction marks.	Untoward saddle movement across the back will cause friction.

Palpation	Response
Near-side head Place palpatory hand on top of poll. Open hand to apply medium pressure from thumb either side of poll.	Some reaction: do again. No reaction: leave. Violent reaction: test other side **(2)**.
Base neck Right hand palpates down base of neck from wither to shoulder, medium pressure.	Horse reacts by moving away **(3)**; you feel a hard lump of resistance. May be muscle tension or compensation for lameness. Seek advice.

2

3

45

be correctly fitted so it does not cause restriction or pain, and it must be maintained properly. If it is not correctly fitted, and if the carriage is not balanced, it will put excessive strain on the horse pulling it, and will also cause him postural and occupational stresses.

Signs of a problem developing include:
- Excessive movement of the saddle to one side, despite all attempts to correct it.
- Saddle slips back persistently, due to a change in the horse's posture.

- Bridging through centre of saddle from loss of muscle contact or loss of flocking.

To be able to detect a problem developing, use the palpatory examination described in Evaluation of the Normal Horse, page 22. A simple exploratory examination takes only a few minutes and can be done on a daily basis, perhaps after exercise (**4–6**). First remove the saddle or harness, and then proceed to examine the horse from head to tail, as described in the accompanying table.

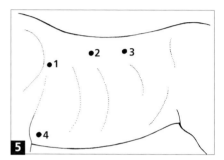

Above: Areas of palpation after removal of saddle
1: behind the scapula
2: angle of top rib
3: back of saddle area
4: girth area

OBSERVATION	INTERPRETATION
Saddle area	
Right hand strokes, medium pressure, where saddle/harness pad sits behind shoulder blade (**4**).	Acute muscle tightening; hollows back and lifts head.
Right hand strokes, medium pressure, down chest wall into girth area (**6**).	Reaction initially slight twitching, becomes more aggressive (turns to bite).
Right hand medium pressure across back muscles towards quarters.	Sinks to ground; moves away. Horse needs further evaluation to determine cause and diagnosis.
Hindquarters	
Palpate with right hand across rump, medium pressure.	Stamps leg.
Down hind leg using cat's paw technique, medium pressure.	Muscle very taut and sensitive. Horse needs evaluation.
Limbs	
Palpate legs all over to feel for lumps, heat, new injuries.	*See* Evaluation of the Normal Horse, pages 23 and 26
Do this first thing in morning and last thing at night. Also good idea to do it after exercise.	

Quick Daily Routine

Finally, for those of you who are very busy and really feel that all you can manage is a quick daily test, then try the following five-minute practical check to identify possible changes in your horse's general well-being. Remember, however, that if your horse appears to be in pain, always call your vet and discuss the matter with him/her. Do not take on the responsibility of diagnosing and treating any problem or disorder yourself: the aim of this chapter is to help you identify abnormal signs in your horse, so that you have a better idea when to seek advice, rather than leaving it to get worse.

ACTION	OBSERVATION
Observe head over door.	Note demeanour; look for signs of respiratory distress and illness (dull eye).
Move horse back from door.	Observe mobility, particularly of stifles.
Check feed/hay/water consumption.	Is horse eating and drinking well?
Observe rugs (blankets) and state of stable (stall).	Has he been cast/is he distressed?
Put headcollar (halter) on.	Is he worried when you touch his head and ears?
Remove rugs (blankets).	Is he irritable/are there signs of injury? Lift tail from fillet string to assess spinal mobility.
Pick up feet to remove bedding.	Note ease of handling, state of feet; observe smell.
Move over in box (stall) sideways.	Note his co-ordination and balance.

47

Management Strategy

In large yards (stables) where many people come in contact with horses, an idea for continuity of care and communication is to set up a daily activity sheet for each horse; these can be held in the office or feed room or pinned up outside the stable area. As an owner this can be reassuring, because it gives you the feeling of being more closely involved – yet you are not bothering anyone by asking all those questions which are interesting to you but slightly irritating to others.

It is also useful when you have several horses and their needs are changing and developing on a daily basis. And it helps the single owner to remember all those important dates, to identify the needs of their horse, and be aware of any potential problems.

EXAMPLE OF DAILY ACTIVITY SHEET

NAME OF HORSE: BEN	DATE: 5/6/00	GROOM: ZOE
Feed x 3	7am 3lb oats 12pm 2lb chaff/1lb nuts (pellets) 6pm 5lb oats	
Exercise	9.30am 3pm	
	1 hour hacking 1 hour jumping lesson	
	Lunge 15 mins before lesson	
Turn out	Midday for 2 hours	
Turn-out boots	No	
Rugs	Fly sheet on	
Saddle	General purpose	
	Stubben jumping	
Girth	As for saddles	
Bridle – bit	Kimblewick for show-jumping and French link for hacking	
Lunging equipment	Cavesson and roller	
Protective boots	Exercise boots + over-reach for S/J	
Special requirements	Massage hindquarters before S/J, and lunge	
	After lunge do stretching exercises x 5 on both hind legs. Hold 20 secs	
Grooming	Pull mane today	
Bandages in stable	Not in day. All round at night	
Temperature	Normal 38°C (100°F)	
Water consumption	Night, 1 bucket	
	Day, 2 buckets	
Electrolytes	Salt in feed 1 tsp x 1 (am)	
Hay	Ad lib soaked	
Stable rugs (blankets)	Light cotton sheet day, crossovers	
	Stable rug (blanket) night, cross-overs	
	Sweat rug (blanket) after work	
Weekly plan	Farrier Thursday 2pm	
	Physical therapist for massage Friday 4pm	
	Lesson flatwork Tues 7pm	

MONTHLY PLAN	DATE	REQUIREMENTS
Competitions		
Schooling		
Farrier		
Vet visit		
Saddler		
Worming		
Physical therapist		
Other		

Preventing Problems

There are several management issues that contribute to the overall success and well-being of you and your horse: dental care, feet and the farrier, nutrition, tack, veterinary assistance – and finally your own fitness as rider or driver.

Regular dental care is essential to the horse's welfare: without an efficient set of teeth he will lose body condition, and any pain caused by sharp hooks and/or sore gums will lead to all sorts of behavioural problems. Diet, too, is fundamental to good health and performance, and a well thought out, consistent nutritional regime will prevent metabolic disorder and loss of capability.

Equally a good farrier is an essential member of your team. If the horse's foot is out of balance it cannot work correctly and then adverse changes will develop, not just in the foot but all the way up the leg, which will quite quickly affect the horse's whole way of going, and his attitude, too.

Well fitting tack is essential to good performance: badly fitting tack, and especially the saddle, can lead to serious muscle damage that inevitably has repercussions throughout the horse's body.

Another important member of the horse's management team is the veterinary surgeon: he/she is trained not just to diagnose and treat injury or illness, but to assess and advise on general care, and thereby help you to maximise your horse's potential.

Finally, don't forget yourself: unfit, stiff and tense, and riding badly, you will not help your horse. This chapter suggests a regime of exercises to improve your own fitness.

The Mouth and Teeth

It is extremely important to have your horse's mouth checked at least twice a year by a veterinary surgeon or a dental technician recommended by your vet. Many performance problems – including head shaking, running off and mouth resistance – can be attributed to pain or malfunction in this area; and without a well functioning set of teeth the horse's health will suffer – he will lose condition due to incorrect chewing action and therefore ineffective utilisation of feedstuffs.

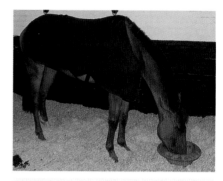

TIP: Feed off the floor so that the horse's teeth can function correctly in opposition.

THE STRUCTURE OF THE MOUTH
The Incisors

The function of these teeth is to cut grass. A normal horse when at rest standing will appear to have its upper jaw protruding 2mm over the lower; however, when it puts its head to the ground to eat, the lower jaw actually comes forwards and the teeth of the upper and lower jaws then meet exactly. It is therefore essential to put all food on the floor, including hay.

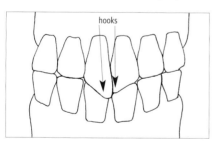

Incisors preventing jaw excursion. The upper jaw will over shoot the lower with the end result of loss of backward and forward movement of the jaw

The Tushes

The tushes are really vestigial tusks, and appear very early when the horse is just a few months old, in the upper and lower jaws. They have no use, but can cause problems by becoming too large or by growing at an angle causing pressure on the cheek or tongue. Sometimes if they are slow to come through, the bit might press on the gum over the tush, causing pain.

Premolars and Molars

The molar teeth are divided into premolars and molars. Some horses grow a wolf tooth, a small tooth on the top jaw; it is in fact the first premolar, and it can interfere with the bit, causing discomfort (see centre, page 51). The molars extend along the upper and lower jaw, and are large in size and number.

Bars

The bars are the areas of gum which overlie the bone between the molars and the incisors; they are very sensitive and can be easily traumatised by severe bitting and/or harsh riding practice.

DENTAL CARE

Regular dental checks are vital for the care of the teeth and re-alignment of the jaw, in order to allow optimum food conversion, and so the horse accepts the bit and establishes a good head carriage. Remember that a horse's teeth keep growing throughout his life, and

PREVENTING PROBLEMS

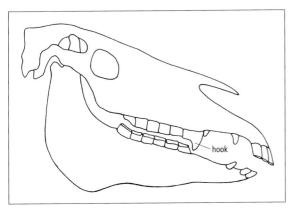

Above: Hooks can develop on the second upper premolars and back molars inhibiting correct movement of the jaw and causing the horse to have problems in chewing

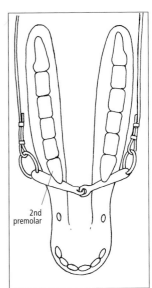

Above: The bit can become caught under the front of the 2nd premolar. This traps the gum between the bit and tooth, causing pain

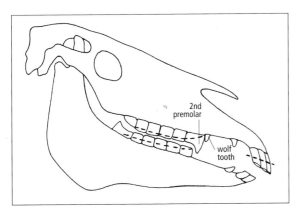

Above and right: To alleviate the problem shown above (top right) the wolf teeth are removed and the 2nd premolar is rasped away to produce a 'bit seat'

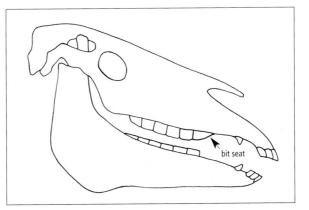

the way his jaw operates can affect their shape, with potentially serious consequences.

To explain: the lower jaw moves forwards as the horse puts its head to the floor and bites the grass; it also moves from side to side as he chews the food and passes it back. This side-to-side and forwards movement is called an excursion. You can test this yourself by parting his lips and lifting his head up and then moving the bottom jaw from side to side. If the distance moved to the left and right is not the same or too little, then there is a problem. Basically, as a result of the forward and backward movement of the lower jaw, hooks may develop on the second upper premolar, and this will then inhibit the forward movement of the lower jaw against the upper jaw.

Because of this restriction in movement, the molar furthest back on the lower jaw will also develop a hook which then prevents the lower jaw moving forwards. As well as normal jaw movement being lost, the molar hooks may well dig into the gums causing pain, and therefore mouth resistance. These developing hooks should be removed and the teeth correctly realigned.

Note, too, that if a horse loses an incisor or a molar tooth, the tooth on the opposite jaw will continue to grow into the gap to such an extent that it may pierce the gum; it will also stop backward and forward side-to-side jaw excursion.

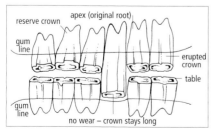

Unopposed teeth. Regular checks will identify if this situation is developing due to a lost tooth on the opposite side

Wolf Teeth

These are the first premolars, normally only occurring in the upper jaw. They are present at birth, and can erupt from a yearling upwards, and vary in size from 1mm to 1cm in length. They can be 2cm or so in front of the second premolar, but are usually adjacent to it, and can be a particular problem when they are on the inside and close to the front of the second premolar. Wolf teeth can be a nuisance and if so should be removed – however, this should only be done by a veterinarian, because if it is not done properly, roots may be left behind.

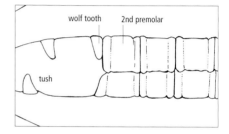

Wolf teeth can cause problems. Always have a veterinary surgeon check them.

Second Premolar

This is the first *large* premolar tooth occurring on each side of both the upper and lower jaw. The bit can become caught against the front of this premolar, trapping the gum, in which instance its front aspect may have to be filed off to allow the bit to fit comfortably.

CONCLUSIONS

Dental correction and realignment will inevitably benefit the horse's general welfare: it will improve food conversion and so help him maintain condition, and it should help to resolve mouth-related behavioural problems. One area that can definitely improve is his head carriage, and thus his action because he will become more forward going, with better engagement.

The Foot

The foot has evolved to bear the horse's weight. It is also required to reduce concussion and promote circulation, and its outer structure must protect sensitive internal structures. The shape of the hoof will vary slightly depending on the nature of the forces placed upon it.

It is very important to maintain the feet well: this means providing good quality dry bedding; a good diet to promote healthy growth; and adequate movement to encourage circulation and to correct mechanical stimulation. Beware of horn preservatives: it has been shown that some may cause problems by working their way into the surface layers causing damage to the horn, so only use them when absolutely necessary.

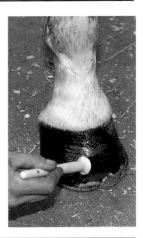

MOVEMENTS OF THE HOOF CAPSULE

During weight-bearing, the downward force on the pedal bone causes the ground surface of the hoof wall to spread. The front two-thirds of the foot are restricted from spreading because of the attachment of the hoof wall to the pedal bone; however, the back third of the foot has no such bony support, and the cartilages, bars and bulbs of the heel allow the foot to spread.

The movements of the hoof wall help to absorb concussion and to pump blood along the veins as well. When observing the foot shape you will notice that the front feet are more circular than the hind feet. In a normal foot, both front feet would match, as would both hind feet. Uneven feet can be caused by an injury or by disease which has promoted uneven weight-bearing and wear, causing size and shape differences.

If the horse is born with odd feet, there is little that can be done after eighteen months of age. Incorrect farriery can also lead to asymmetry of foot shape, as can negligence of regular trimming.

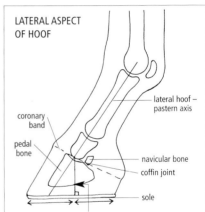

LATERAL ASPECT OF HOOF

lateral hoof – pastern axis

coronary band

pedal bone

navicular bone

coffin joint

sole

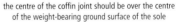

the centre of the coffin joint should be over the centre of the weight-bearing ground surface of the sole

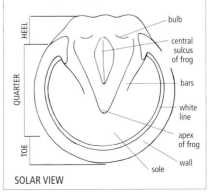

bulb

central sulcus of frog

bars

white line

apex of frog

wall

sole

HEEL

QUARTER

TOE

SOLAR VIEW

Hoof Balance

If the foot cannot work correctly, then adverse changes will develop. These are brought about in the main by incorrect foot balancing caused by infrequent trimming or shoeing, or poor quality of farriery. However, to be really aware of the internal alignment of the foot – which it is necessary to trim and shoe correctly – radiographs may be required.

PREVENTING PROBLEMS

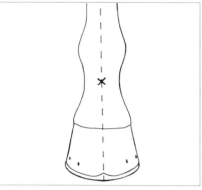

Normal foot viewed from the front

An imaginary vertical line should extend down from the centre of the fetlock joint to the centre of the toe. The toe should point forwards, and there should be an even amount of foot on either side of the line.

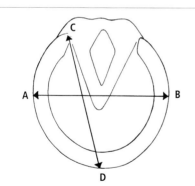

Solar Surface

On the solar surface, line A–B should equal the length of line C–D.

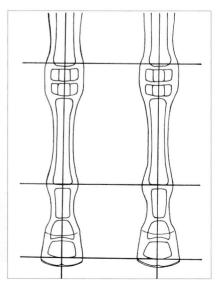

Medio-lateral foot balance

The ground surface of the foot should be in parallel with the centre of the fetlock joints in both the front and hind legs, and in parallel with the upper knee and upper hock joints.

Incorrect Hoof Balance

In the front feet, a long toe with low heels **(1)** will increase the load taken by the flexor tendons and the accessory check ligament; this will eventually cause the horse to alter his posture and change his gait.

As a result of change in the lateral angles of the feet, there will also be gait changes, and then restrictions to blood flow in the back third of the foot. The end result is lameness. The hind limb which has an incorrect pastern–hoof axis puts strain on the suspensory ligament and causes gait changes and other upper limb and spinal compensatory problems.

Changes in medio-lateral hoof balance will put strain on the fetlock joints, and will ultimately displace the coronary band.

TIP: Using studs on one side can also cause this imbalance and should be avoided.

FOUR-POINT SHOEING AND TRIMMING

Four-point shoeing **(2)** has been developed and applied to our horses as a result of looking more closely at the feet of feral horses living in varying environmental conditions. In the unshod horse turned out in fields we may also see similarities to the four-point trim concept, for he is shaping his own foot using his bodyweight.

When it comes to shoeing, there have always been wide variances amongst farriers and veterinarians world wide as to what constitutes 'normal'. The four-point shoe or trim is also subjected to these variances of

1

The white limb demonstrates a low heel and longer toe

2

normal, the main mistake appearing to be that farriers are taking off too much horn and then using the four-point break-over. Where this has not worked, it may be because of this misunderstanding.

Most cases of horn failure that have occurred as a result of faulty mechanics, could have been prevented, largely through the implementing of improved environmental conditioning and mechanics. As well as being used in cases of structural horn failure and foot lameness, four-point shoeing and trimming helps to produce a better foot. The four-point trim and shoeing technique offers protection, and enhances rapid growth of horn and sole: the entire hoof capsule can be replaced in 6–8 months as opposed to 12–14 months. The four-point method allows the break-over point to be forward of the apex of the frog, and the heel loading close to the widest point of the frog: this gives full use of the natural load zones, and so stimulates horn growth.

Radiographs have to be taken to identify the shape and location of the coffin bone and how it relates to the ground surface, as well as its anterior/posterior and medial/lateral balance. It also gives important information on the sole depth.

A point to remember is that the hoof capsule does not always coincide with the internal balance, and only radiographs can confirm this. At the end of the day, the internal balance and horn mass determines soundness and the potential to heal.

Nutrition

Diet is fundamental to performance and the horse's general well-being, and a consistent, well thought out nutritional regime will help to prevent metabolic problems and loss of performance. To a large extent a horse's digestive system relies on the activity of the microbial population in the hindgut, and any sudden change in diet, or excessive feeding of starchy cereals, will upset its equilibrium and could lead to colic and/or laminitis. The horse has evolved as a 'trickle' feeder, and for optimum health he needs to be eating a highly fibrous diet almost continuously (18 hours per day).

We should also pay more attention to the labels on the bags of food and supplements we buy, so that we understand more exactly what we are feeding. By understanding more fully a horse's daily requirements, we should be able to assess how much we should be feeding him (weight), what type of feed (forage and/or cereals), and whether he needs any supplements (vitamin, mineral). We should take into account the horse's pasture, too, because some areas are deficient in certain trace elements and minerals, and this can have a deleterious effect on his well-being. Take a soil sample and have it analysed to find out if you need to feed vitamin and/or mineral supplements. Nowadays, expert nutritional advice is easily available to us all in the form of seminars, magazines, books and help-lines; there are also nutritionists and, of course, your veterinarian, and I would strongly suggest that if you have any doubts or queries regarding diet and/or feedstuffs, you ask their advice.

TIP: If you feed your horse less than the manufacturer recommends for the amount of work he is doing, you may need to supplement his diet with appropriate vitamins and minerals.

ESSENTIAL NUTRIENTS

These include protein, carbohydrates, fats, minerals, vitamins and water. A horse's nutrient requirements will vary during his life in response to growth and workload. Exercise increases the requirements of some, for example carbohydrates and fats to provide energy, and water and electrolytes to replace losses in sweat.

Minerals

These are inorganic substances involved in many bodily functions. They are very important in exercise in maintaining osmotic pressure, fluid balance and the activity of the nervous and muscular systems. Minerals (electrolytes) are lost in sweating, and losses may be high in excessive situations and must therefore be replaced in the form of electrolytes. Minerals cannot be stored in the body, and those excess to the horse's requirements are excreted in the urine – so make sure he has plenty of water. Be careful not to over-feed minerals, because over-feeding one mineral may affect the absorption of another – for example, too much zinc affects calcium and copper absorption.

Vitamins

These are organic substances produced in the body or absorbed in food; the horse's needs vary according to age, workload and how he is managed – for instance, if he is stabled for long periods he will probably need supplements.

Water

Free access to clean, fresh water is essential at all times. Water accounts for 70 per cent of the horse's total bodyweight, and is required for all metabolic processes. When

levels, use cereal grains and supplemented fat. Fat is more efficiently converted into usable energy than hay and cereals; it also reduces the heat load effect, and is therefore especially useful in hot and humid conditions. The best way to give fat or oil in the diet is in the form of corn or soya oil. (It is recommended that additional vitamin E be fed in combination with supplemental oil – seek expert advice on this.) Because fat increases the energy density of the feed, more fibre can be fed, and you can reduce the cereal content; it also means the horse can eat less without compromising his needs – which is useful if you have a fussy eater.

water is lost as sweat, it must be replaced to prevent dehydration: a 3 per cent loss of bodyweight from sweating is enough to affect performance – endurance horses can lose 5–10 per cent of their bodyweight.

MANAGEMENT ISSUES

In winter, feed plenty of good quality hay: it is converted into energy more slowly than cereals, and so is good for 'internal heating'. Hay as fibre is also essential to maintain a healthy hind gut and assist fluid exchange.

If you need to increase the horse's energy

Feed cereals and/or concentrates in small amounts and at frequent intervals because the horse has a small, relatively inelastic stomach, and a limited capacity to digest starch in the small intestine. This will reduce the likelihood of colic and/or laminitis.

Signs that the horse does not feel well include the following: loss of appetite; dull, lifeless coat; stiffness; eating droppings/tree bark; excessive sweating; over-excited, hyperactivity; lethargy; muscle problems. These should be discussed with your veterinarian.

Tack

Correctly measured shoes and appropriate equipment is essential to the success of the human athlete: so how often could it be that inappropriate and poorly fitting tack is the cause of poor performance in our horse? In many cases horses are sold on because of unsatisfactory results, indeed some even become lame. Yet if their tack were to fit properly their performance could be restored and enhanced.

With tack that fits comfortably the horse can move freely and without impingement or pain, and therefore performs to his best ability. A correctly fitted saddle allows the rider to be balanced and centred on the horse, and does not interfere with the horse's movement; similarly a bit that allows a horse to work comfortably can only encourage a better performance.

HOW YOU AS OWNER/RIDER CAN HELP

- Try to learn as much as you can about fitting tack correctly.
- Be tolerant to the fact that it can take time to sort out some saddles.
- Work your horse correctly to develop a strong outline and good muscle tone.
- Be prepared to involve the veterinary surgeon to identify lameness, and to advise therapy if it is appropriate.
- Be fair to your horse and your saddler. If the saddle that fitted your old horse is two sizes different for the new one, you really cannot expect your saddler to be able to make it fit.
- Do not follow trends and fashion: think sensibly, and seek professional advice – and then follow it.

Well fitting tack allows the horse to move freely and gives the rider maximum performance potential

The Bridle and Bit

THE BRIDLE

The bridle must hold the bit centrally in the mouth, in the gap between the canines and second premolars. Too high and tight and it will pinch the corners of the lips; too low – as some Western riders tend to fit it – and it will hit against the canine teeth, and also move too much when the rider takes up the contact with the reins.

The browband and headpiece must allow enough room to accommodate the front and top of the head comfortably, and not pinch them; they should not ride up behind the ears too tightly. This can cause symptoms ranging from head tossing to a tilted head carriage.

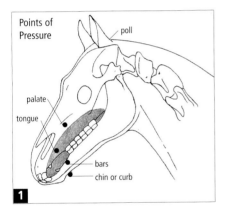

Points of Pressure

poll

palate

tongue

bars

chin or curb

1

THE BIT

If the bit is incorrectly fitted it can cause many different problems. There may be pain from impingement or bruising, causing the horse to fuss in his mouth or even to run away, the overall picture being of an obviously uncomfortable animal. He will end up moving abnormally, and the stress and trauma could well cause compensatory problems in other areas. One solution might be to try a bit that allowed the tongue more freedom **(4&5)**, perhaps one with a port: the horse would

2

A joint adds a nutcracker effect to the action of the bit

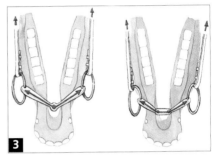

3

Arrows indicate the direction of pressure of snaffle (left) and French-link (right) bits. They act on the tongue and corners of the month

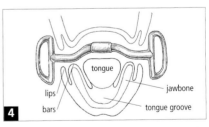

tongue

lips

jawbone

bars

tongue groove

4

Myler bit. This design allows the horse to respond to pressure on the bit and then seeking relief he relaxes at the poll and brings his head down to a 90° angle with the ground

5

A Sprenger ported snaffle that allows the tongue more freedom

problems with breathing, and the horse's performance will almost certainly be affected. However, it has recently been observed that some horses can race more efficiently – often faster and with more stamina – if they are ridden in a bitless bridle. One such bridle has been developed in association with a veterinary surgeon in the USA and is currently marketed as the Spirit bridle.

Driving horses often suffer just as much abuse. Many driving bits are straight-bar (8), and often the horse

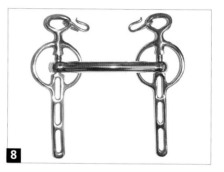

become more supple in his jaw and associated musculature as a result of a comfortable and relaxed tongue, and so would move more freely through his neck and shoulders. Look at Western riding (6): typically this uses a light rein contact and a bit with a port, and as a result you rarely see resistance in the horse's mouth – his movement is therefore invariably more fluent and pleasing.

Sometimes the horse is caused discomfort by his owner's malpractice. The English riding style asks for more collection and therefore more contact, but if the horse shows resistance in his mouth he is then very often ridden in a noseband which attempts to keep his mouth shut, such as a grakle (figure-eight) or flash (7) – and if his teeth need attention and are not in alignment, then the effects of a tight noseband are even worse. Ultimately this could cause inflammation and pain in the joints of the jaw, leading to stiffness in the neck and difficulty in flexing. This will all lead to problems elsewhere in the spine, and the horse's movement will deteriorate. These particular symptoms might be confused with those caused by an ill-fitting saddle, rather than dental problems, so be sure to have his mouth checked, too.

Some racehorses have a tendency to swallow their tongue, or to loll it out to one side when racing, and to prevent this it is tied down. This can cause further discomfort and

seems to find such a bit restrictive, particularly in inexperienced or harsh hands; I have seen many horses apparently holding their breath, and indeed their tongues have become blue from the pressure of the bit. Inevitably this will cause behavioural and schooling problems.

A relaxed and pleasing picture with a well fitted, uncomplicated bridle

Saddles

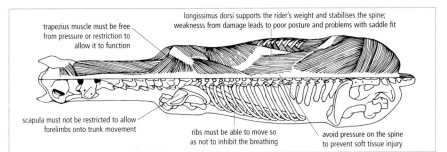

trapezius muscle must be free from pressure or restriction to allow it to function

longissimus dorsi supports the rider's weight and stabilises the spine; weaknesss from damage leads to poor posture and problems with saddle fit

scapula must not be restricted to allow forelimbs onto trunk movement

ribs must be able to move so as not to inhibit the breathing

avoid pressure on the spine to prevent soft tissue injury

Saddles come in different sizes – as in lengths and widths – and in many styles: Western; show jumping; event; dressage; GP (general purpose); hunter/show; and pony. If at all possible each horse should have his own saddle which has been measured to fit. The saddle should be checked at the end of the winter and in the early autumn for any defects to its shape, and to assess if the horse has changed in his muscle or postural development and wither fitting. Where there are several horses and the saddles are shared, each horse should be assessed and the saddle of nearest fit chosen from your selection. This requires having a certain knowledge of tree shape and width, and of the horse's width and spinal shape. It is also important that the horse can move to his best ability in the saddle you provide, and also that you can ride in it safely and effectively.

Different tree shapes can cause problems. For instance, the Western saddle tends to have a long, flat tree, and this may put undue

pressure on the withers and over the loins, with relatively little support in the middle. The dressage saddle is sometimes designed with an excessively curved tree and seat **(1)** to help the rider

maintain a better position – but this is with little regard for the actual anatomy of the horse, since this excessive curve can cause pressure points through the centre whilst the back of the saddle is hardly in contact with the horse's back at all. This means the rider's weight is not evenly distributed and overloads certain soft tissues, leading to circulatory changes and permanent cellular damage.

If a horse specialises in a particular discipline, he should be correctly fitted with a specialist saddle by a professional, and that saddle used for the rest of his competitive life, including his training.

2

CORRECT SADDLE FIT (2)

In order to evaluate whether your saddle fits correctly you first need to assess your horse's shape and conformation. This includes:

- the length of his back
- the symmetry of his muscles
- his width

- the shape of his abdomen
- the job the saddle has to do

The saddle has to allow the horse full movement through his back, so that the muscles can expand and contract freely: so a symmetrical, balanced saddle is very important. It might be an idea to ask your saddler to drop out the saddle's panels so he can look at its internal symmetry, and to check the attachment of the girth straps, and potential pressure points from tree and stirrup points. Internal asymmetry can cause severe soft tissue damage, and lead to violent behaviour.

The girth should lie at the narrowest point of the ribcage and perpendicular to the ground

forwards onto the shoulder blades: move the girth to the correct position to resolve this.

Note that a dressage girth can cause discomfort if it attaches just behind the horse's elbow. This would be too short: it would be better for the buckles to end up just below the saddle, out of the way of the rider's leg and the horse's elbow.

SADDLE EXAMINATION WITH THE RIDER

Where possible use a mounting block so as to avoid twisting the saddle tree and hurting your horse's back. When mounting, the right hand should never pull on the cantle because this creates a twisting motion through the saddle and could damage it permanently: place your right hand on the right side behind the pommel. Once mounted, assess the saddle position by first riding up and down in a straight line, then in a circle.

Points to Check

- The clearance of the saddle over the withers.
- Its position: is it central on the horse's back?
- Its stability: it should not rock, or move up and down at the back, or from side to side.
- Your position: are you level (not collapsing hip, riding with one stirrup leather longer)?
- Do you have a problem in the shoulders/hips/back/other joints which may cause weakness or tilting?

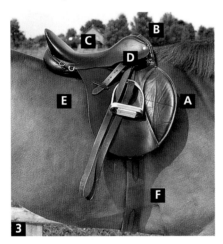

Saddle fitting checkpoints:
A: Sits behind shoulder blade
B: Good clearance of withers and through spine
C: Level seat and sitting on horse's back all way through. Good panel contact.
D: Correct width fitting
E: Not too long. Not extending beyond last rib of horse
F: Girth should not be too short, to avoid buckles impinging on the elbow

CORRECT GIRTH POSITION

The girth should hold the saddle in the correct position on the horse's back; it should lie at the narrowest point of the ribcage and perpendicular to the ground. In some horses the girth line is just behind the elbow; however, most are 6–10cm (3–4in) behind it. If the girth slips forwards whilst riding it will pull the saddle

Saddle Fitting Problems

If you are looking at a horse for the first time you will be able to detect abnormalities in the tissues that may help to identify a saddle problem. Equally you should be diligently casting an eye over your own horse regularly in order to pick up the first signs of damage. The following are some detectable signs of damage:

- sores
- white hairs **(1)**
- temporary swellings (on removing saddle) **(2)**
- scars
- hard spots
- wastage of muscles – the trapezius and longissimus dorsal muscles will be affected
- areas of increased sensitivity: these are called trigger points

The following are behavioural problems that might well arise in the horse because of a badly fitting saddle:

- Objection to being saddled.
- Violent reaction when the girth is tightened – falling over, rearing.
- Biting or tail swishing when the saddle is put in place or when he is girthed up.
- Severe sweating in the area of the saddle.
- Increased sensitivity and discomfort in the girth or saddle area.
- Will not stand still when the rider tries to mount.
- Reacts badly when the rider's foot is placed in the stirrup.
- 'Cold backed' – the horse dips his back away from saddle pressure, or humps it against it.
- Obvious resistance in his work: not going forwards; not happy in transitions up or down; bucking on landing after a jump; shuffling/tripping.

This shows bad practice: wherever possible, use a mounting block to avoid damage to the saddle *and* the horse

Saddle Positioning and Fit

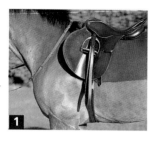

TOO FAR FORWARDS (1&2)

The rider will be sitting on the horse's shoulder. The saddle will twist from left to right across the spine as each shoulder moves. Note that a Western saddle can put enormous pressure on the top of the shoulder blades.

POMMEL TOO HIGH

The saddle may be too narrow if you can fit more than three fingers between the withers and the pommel when the rider is in the saddle; he or she will have the feeling of riding uphill. Their weight will be tipped to the back of the saddle and this can cause bruising and damage to the muscles. The horse will be unable to use his back correctly, and will tend to run away from the discomfort with his head held unnaturally high.

POMMEL TOO LOW (3)

The saddle is either too wide, or it needs reflocking; sometimes the horse is lacking in muscle, and this needs to be developed first. If the saddle is too wide, the rider's weight will be tipped forwards and their legs backwards.

BRIDGING

The saddle should be in contact all along the horse's back. To test this, girth the saddle up, being sure to use the first and third girth straps so that the saddle is anchored from front and back, and check with the flat of your hand and fingers that the saddle does lie in contact all the way through, and that no daylight can be seen under the panels. If the saddle lifts up at the back, then this particular horse may need a saddle that has a deeper gusset or a flatter panel in the waist of the saddle.

If you can detect a loss of contact through the centre of the panels then he may have muscle damage or weakness causing a loss of muscle. Alternatively the saddle may need reflocking at this point **(4)**.

TWISTING TO ONE SIDE

The saddle may not be symmetrical: if it is heavier on one side than the other, it will shift to the heavier side. Or the horse may be less well developed behind the shoulder blade and wither on one side: this would cause the saddle to fall into the space. Or the horse is lame, causing too much movement to one side.

PREVENTING PROBLEMS

Saddle Fitting

TIP: Note that some Master Saddlers are only qualified to make saddles, they are not necessarily qualified to fit them: fitting is another qualification altogether. So when you contact a Master Saddler with a view to purchasing a new saddle, make sure he is trained in fitting it, too.

Left: The panels on this saddle are totally different: the left is wider and less flocked than the right

PROBLEM	CAUSE
Saddle moves forwards or back.	Saddle and/or girth may have been placed too far back/forwards.
Slides from side to side.	Tree may be too narrow.
	Saddle may be too far forwards.
Saddle rises excessively to one side.	Over-development of shoulder muscle on one side.
	One stirrup may be longer than the other.
	Horse may be lame
	Manufacturing or flocking defect may be making saddle asymmetric.
Saddle not in contact: rocks and rises up at the back.	Saddle too wide.
	Panels too curved, causing rocking over a central point.

CONFORMATIONAL PROBLEMS	SOLUTION
Horse with the narrowest part of chest behind his elbow: causes saddle to slide forwards.	Use the girth straps towards the front of the saddle
Narrowest part of his chest is further back: the saddle slides back.	Use the girth straps towards the back of the saddle.
High-withered horses.	Use a thick panel to lift the saddle up and over the withers; seek professional remedial saddler's help.
Most exercise and racing saddles have a half tree or no tree at all: these will sit directly on the horse's spine or cause friction at the end of the half tree.	Use a saddle with a full tree and under-gullet.
Long withers ie they extend further back than is usual.	Needs special attention to stop the saddle hitting the spine in front of the saddle.
Swaybacked horse: the cause may be trauma, conformation, or old age.	Remedy posture and muscle development if possible; it may be necessary to use a shorter tree and panels to fit.

Saddle Pads and Numnahs

Very often a numnah (shaped saddle pad) is used to keep the saddle clean. It should not be used as a substitute for a well fitting saddle, nor should it try and mask problems in the saddle. Unfortunately numnahs and pads are often sold as being able to prevent and correct back problems in the horse when this is actually an impossibility. However, because saddles are very expensive and some horses are difficult to fit, owners are persuaded to buy all sorts of numnahs that claim unproven facts. Most important, a numnah should be large enough, and preferably shaped, so that it can be pulled well up into the gullet of the saddle and therefore not cause any pressure

to bear on the spine, or friction across the horse's back. A numnah or pad is certainly of benefit when used to help position the saddle evenly whilst a horse builds up muscle in the event of his being one-sided; however, its continuing use must be carefully monitored.

Note that Western saddles are designed to be used with a pad because the bars are only covered with a layer of sheepskin and have no cushioning.

In certain situations a horse's performance will be greatly improved when a numnah is used; however, beware that you are not masking a problem temporarily that in the long term will re-appear, possibly in another area. For example, placing a pad under the saddle can cause it to shift position, so all you are doing is moving the pressure points to a different area – although the horse may improve initially, the fundamental problem has not been alleviated. Computerised saddle pressure analysis has confirmed that the addition of thick pads generally

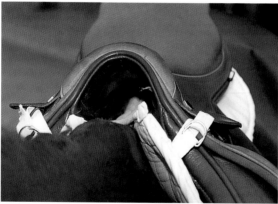

Always check for clearance of the spine. This shows a spineless numnah which requires care in fitting to avoid pressure points

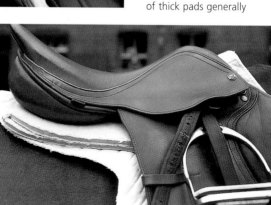

Some pads can help balance a saddle temporarily, but always consult a saddle fitter to make the adjustment

increases the pressure on each side of the horse's withers; they may also fill the gullet, causing more potential pressure over the spinous processes and soft tissues. So always ensure that before you resort to full-time use of a numnah, you first improve the horse's flexibility and eliminate the cause of the 'cold back', or stiffness, or lack of muscle development.

WATCHPOINT:
- Always call in a qualified saddle fitter to advise you, and show them the numnah that you generally use.
- Check the panels of your saddle regularly yourself for pressure points and loss of cushioning.
- Check numnah edges and fit, and that it clears the spine.

PROBLEM	SOLUTION
Saddle too low at the withers.	Saddler will fit a pad as a temporary aid for the balance of the rider.
Saddle not making contact through centre panels due to lack of muscle.	In the short term use a pad/numnah to 'fill' the interface caused by lack of muscle; in the long term, build up the muscle.

NUMNAH (SADDLE PAD) SOLUTIONS

TYPE	POTENTIAL USE AND PROBLEMS
Cotton square/shape	For everyday and summer use. Check edges and size for potential impingement.
Shock-absorbing	Check it does not bear down on the horse's spine. If it has no anti-shear it can make pressure points worse.
Sheepskin	Good for sweating horses in winter as it 'breathes'.
Synthetic pad	Can make the horse sweat; it might irritate the skin.
Shaped and raised pad. It alters the saddle position by raising it	Check that it allows the spine freedom of movement and does not bear down on the withers. Important to monitor the saddle position over time to check it does not cause saddle position problem.

Right, a well fitted numnah; far right, this is a bad numnah because it is too small, so creating a step and therefore potential movement.

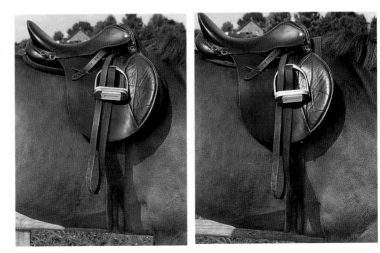

The Rider/Driver

This section concentrates on the rider: it is important to exercise yourself because your bad posture and/or lack of fitness could have a deleterious effect on the way you ride/drive and therefore the horse's performance. Most of us devote a great deal of time and effort to the fitness and well-being of our horses, and hardly spare a thought to our own. However, the quality of our riding directly affects the way in which the horse responds, and the quality of the movement he then produces: any tensions or stiffness on our part will mean that we are not giving the aids evenly and smoothly, so the horse is constantly having to interpret messages that are slightly different each time.

The reasons for our physical shortcomings will be many and various. Many of us will have suffered tissue and muscle trauma from falls, and perhaps damage to bones and joints, too, which inevitably will have restricted our range of movement. Also the nature of our daily work may cause postural and stress-related problems: bent over a desk, hard physical work, riding horses all day.

Most of us have one leg and arm that is stronger than the other, and this can cause a chain of problems. The stronger leg may cause the hip to drop (**see left**), resulting in more weight being put into one seat bone; causing the saddle to move across the horse's spine, and the horse to go crooked. A stronger arm may cause us to collapse, rotate or elevate that shoulder; we

Use a fork that is the right length for *you*; and remember to work from both sides

will then be crooked through our spine and unlevel in our seat, wrists and hands, and this will make it very difficult to maintain a sympathetic rein contact.

Low back stiffness can result in decreased pelvic mobility and leg flexibility, reducing the overall strength and suppleness of the seat. This in turn may hinder the horse's own natural flexibility. How we hold our head and neck also significantly affects how we move through the rest of our body – the human head can weigh up to 10–14lb so it is essential to maintain an upright posture.

A canter pirouette. Maximum rider posture helps give the best possible performance

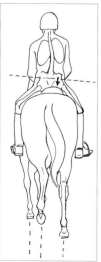

Rider Position

TIP: If you can't get your stirrups level and you ride asymmetrically, have your leg length checked by a specialist; he or she will help you to resolve any significant discrepancy through physiotherapy and stretching.

COMMON FAULTS	REMEDY
Neck & Head	
Jutting chin forwards.	Check hat fit/tightness of chinstrap.
Tilting head sideways **(1)**.	Learn to be aware of tilt, and correct it. (Try looking straight through horse's ears.)
Nodding head.	Backward-tilting pelvis.
Too still and erect: forced stiff-necked appearance.	Learn to release head and neck.
Shoulders	
Rounding, hunching **(2)**.	Causes: bad posture adopted at work has become a norm; reins too short. Remedy: bring arm back to point where upper arm is perpendicular. Stretch strapping tape across the back of shoulders – when you slump, it will pull.
Dropped or raised on one side.	Check neck, and muscular tone of neck and shoulder muscles. Learn body awareness. May be mid-, low back problem.
Arms and Hands	
Arms locked straight and shoulders rounded **(3)**. Hands turned inwards and elbows outwards.	Correct hand position: make sure thumbs are uppermost. Elbow and wrist and finger joints should be supple. Hands should be held with thumbs uppermost and wrists very slightly rounded inwards. If you find this difficult, check spinal and peripheral limb suppleness.

PREVENTING PROBLEMS

Riders who spend many hours riding, and who take little other form of exercise, will probably suffer back ache, and in time decreased flexibility. It is therefore important to devote time to other ranges of movement. A structured regime of remedial and fitness exercises can only improve our riding and so benefit our horses.

The Legs Weakness in legs, leading to instability in rider's overall position **(4)**.	Lack of muscle tone and hip tightness: develop 'core' stability of abdominal and pelvic muscles and so improve flexibility of all low back and pelvic/leg muscles.
Balance Rider tips forwards (can be anxiety, nervousness). Collapsing in front and rounding back **(2)**.	Increase confidence. Insuffient stomach muscle tone and low back stiffness. Remedy by increasing tone, and seek advice for low back flexibility.
Reins too short.	Lengthen reins. Can be caused by rider anxiety, so build up confidence.
Asymmetry Rider collapses hip, so more weight in one seat bone than the other **(5)**.	Check low back and pelvis.
Collapses hip and seat slides out to opposite side.**(6)**	Check leg/stirrup length.
Whole body twists to inside. All weight on outside seat bone, so horse will fall out through same shoulder.	Check spinal symmetry and hip flexibility.

70

Good Lifestyle Guide

The Working Environment

- Eye/head height is very important: you should not be obliged to maintain any abnormal flexed posture (looking up or down, head tilted or turned sideways) for any length of time.
- Avoid clasping the telephone in the side of the neck.
- Change visual work from one side to the other at regular intervals so you are not always working from the same side.
- Change body position frequently – avoid sitting for long periods of time.
- Correct body position regularly – relax at regular times during the day, and correct your posture.

In the Stableyard

- Work from both sides of the body, for example when sweeping, mucking out.
- Use a broom, fork etc with a length of handle appropriate for your height.
- Observe correct body posture when lifting *(see* Lifting and Carrying, **1**).
- Do not lift heavy, wet haynets and buckets: steam hay, take buckets to pipes, and use a hose.
- Avoid concussion, and wear good supportive footwear.

Exercise/Fitness

- Warm up your own body properly before you ride/exercise.
- Do other forms of exercise; cardiovascular 3 x 20 mins a week.
- Work the back and hip extensors, and strengthen the abdominals.
- Walk 20 mins per day, and walk wherever possible.

Pre-screening

- See qualified therapist for preventive care.

Other

- Attend meditation/yoga/body awareness clinics, or do home study classes such as Pilates.

Massages

- Have regular sports massage and relaxation massages to aid circulation and decrease potential for stress and loss of tissue extensibility.

Suppling/Stretching

- Do regularly once warmed up to retain tissue length and joint flexibility.

Lifting and Carrying

- Assess weight and size **(2)**.
- Bend knees, keep back straight, head upright, chin in, and exhale on maximum effort.
- Carry close to you.
- To place down, flex knees, keep bottom in, back upright, and exhale as you do so.

1

2

Warm-up Exercises

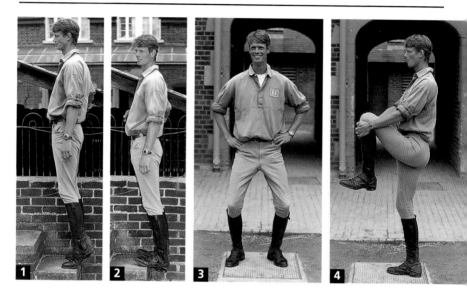

It is important always to warm up well before you do any form of stretching exercise. To warm up, walk briskly and/or walk on the spot, or slow jog on the spot for 5–10 minutes.

Joint Mobility

- Up and down on toes x 5 (**1 and 2**).
- Knee crouches one-third of way slow (keep straight and bottom in), count down to 5 and back up to 5 (repeat 3 times) **(3)**.
- Bring knee up to chest to count of 5 and reverse **(4)**.
- Gently swing leg backwards from hip (tuck bottom in and back straight).

Body and Pelvis

- Draw circles with hips and buttocks in a large circle – knees slightly bent and back upright as you do it **(5)**. Go 3 complete circuits each way.
- Knees slightly flexed and feet apart, slide outside hand down outside of left leg **(6)**. Do to count of 5 and up to count of 5. Repeat other side.

72

7

8

- For extra mobility, bring opposite arm over to same side over head **(7)**. Do exercise x 3 each way.

Shoulders
- Roll backwards and down in gentle circular motion x 3 (both sides together) **(8).**
- Hold upper arm at right angles to body with elbows bent and hands at sternum level, then open out to side to fully extend arm; do x 3 **(9)**.

TIP: Breathe out as you perform the movement.

9

Neck and Head
- Hold chin in and 'grow tall', gently stretching neck at back **(10)** – slowly turn (keep shoulders still) head to left and back to middle, count of 3 and back **(11)**. Do both ways .

After these mobility exercises do a further brisk walk or gentle jog, speeding up towards the end.

10

11

73

STRETCHING

This means holding the end-of-range stretch for 10 secs and then stretching a little more for a further 5/10 secs. **CAUTION:** *no bouncing* at the end of the limit of any stretch. Stretching enables free and easier movement by helping to lengthen the muscles and stimulate the tendons. In this respect, all the major muscle groups should be stretched. If you are aware of stiffness and lack of flexibility doing these exercises, seek further help. *Always* warm up first.

As a general rule, you should do these at least three times a week, with at least five repetitions of each exercise. Do not use trick movements – do them properly.

Single Calf Stretch (12)

- Place one leg behind the other with feet parallel and the back foot flat on the ground.
- Bend the forward knee until you feel a 'pull' on the calf of the back leg.
- Hold to 10, then slowly push a little further and hold for 5–10 seconds. Slowly release.
- Do on the opposite leg.

Soleus Stretch (13)

- Standing with your heels flat on the ground, bend both knees, letting your ankles bend as far as they can while your feet stay flat. Hold to 10, then push a little further and hold for 5–10 seconds. Slowly release.

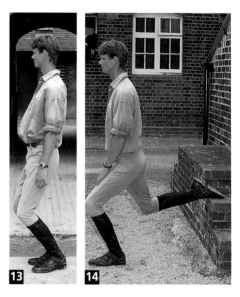

Standing Stretch

- Stand on one leg. Bend the other knee up, holding your ankle behind you with your hand. Pull your heel towards your buttock, keeping your hip well forward until you feel a 'pull' on the front of the thigh; then and push a little further and hold for 5–10 seconds. Alternatively **(14)** instead of holding the ankle, place the toe on a support and bend the opposite knee (see photo). Slowly release.
- Do on opposite leg.

Hamstrings (15)

- Stand on one leg, and place the other straight in front of you on a support; then reach forwards from the hips to hold your foot or ankle, keeping your back straight

TIP: For hamstring stretch, relax knee in slight bend, exhale on stretch forwards (if you can't do the exercises easily with leg on full stretch).

and your head up. Hold to count of 10 and push a little further, then hold for 5–10 seconds more. Slowly release.

- Repeat on other leg.

Alternative Hamstring Stretch (16)

- Stand with feet crossed, close together, keep the front knee pressed straight against the back knee, and bend forwards from the hips.

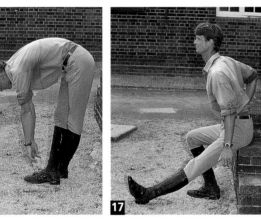

- Hold for 10, then go a little further and hold for 5–10 secs. Slowly release.
- Repeat on other leg.
- Sit on a support **(17)**. Extend one leg out in front of you. Pull toes and foot up towards you.
- Bend slowly forwards from waist. Keep curve in low back.
- Feel stretch up back of straight leg. Hold for 10, then stretch a little more. Hold for 5–10 secs.
- Repeat with other leg.

Adductor Muscle Stretch (18)

- Stretch the left leg straight out sideways, then bend the other knee, until you feel the stretch on your straight leg on inside of thigh.
- Hold to 10, then ask a little more stretch, holding for 5–10 seconds. Slowly release.
- Repeat on other leg.

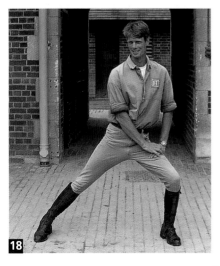

Third Party Care

THE VETERINARY SURGEON

The vet has trained for many years to be able to make a diagnosis based on findings from a thorough examination; he is then able to determine an appropriate treatment regime and management plan to follow. However, many fail to appreciate that his role is not just to diagnose and treat, but, together with the other members of the horse's care team – the farrier, dentist, physical therapist, nutritionist – to provide and advise on general care based on maintenance and prevention, therefore maximising potential and performance. He can also pre-screen the horse for any problems that may not have been identified, therefore reducing the risk of injury and the development of chronic problems.

COMPLEMENTARY THERAPIES

As in human medicine, there are 'alternative' therapies available for horses. They can be distinguished from traditional Western medicine because they treat the patient as a whole being, and not just the individual symptoms of the disease. Unfortunately a great deal of confusion and antipathy has arisen regarding their use, largely because so many unqualified practitioners have set themselves up as experts. In fact in Great Britain this directly contravenes the Veterinary Surgeons Act, which makes it illegal for any person who is not a veterinary surgeon to diagnose and treat any condition or disease, whether by modern drugs or traditional natural medicines. It does, however, allow referral for physiotherapy (this includes osteopathy and chiropractic treatment). In the USA, laws vary state by state. The main problem is that unqualified practitioners will often misdiagnose and give inappropriate treatment, so that although the horse might appear improved, often this is only temporary, and the trouble reappears later on. Increasingly, however, alternative medicine is becoming accepted; some veterinary surgeons practise these themselves, or they have a professional working as part of their team. It is my personal feeling that any horse with a problem should be assessed by the veterinary surgeon together with the complementary therapists for his maximum all-round benefit.

HOMOEOPATHY

This system of medicine looks at exploiting the natural reaction of the body to an external stimulus in order to bring about a healing effect; it works on the principle that 'like cures like' (use arsenic to treat arsenic poisoning). It operates directly on the dynamic and energetic processes of the body, helping to restore normal function. It does not create any residues, which means it can be used safely in competition and on pregnant mares.

MANIPULATIVE THERAPY

Manipulation of the horse is performed by chiropractors, osteopaths and physical therapists; the latter also employ electro-therapy and rehabilitation exercise as part of their treatment approach. The intention of all three is to restore normal musculo-skeletal and neural function. Chiropractors treat problem areas using a high velocity, small amplitude thrust; the osteopath's approach normally involves leverage and torsion, and a low velocity, high amplitude manipulation. Physical therapists work differently, some addressing the muscle imbalance and spinal mobility at the same time, some concentrating on the musculo-skeletal and neural imbalance; they will often look at correcting the underlying problems, and advise on providing the optimum conditions for restoration of normal function.

IMPORTANT: be sure to read the section on Safety on page 88 and the Important Notes on the Use of Massage on page 112 before you start any massage routine

Massage

Massage can be utilised to help counteract the effects of exercise and daily pressures. For many of our animals, stiffness and pain are a way of life to which they have become habituated, and it is often not until you have performed your first massage on your horse that you realise how tight his muscles are, and therefore how much of his energy is consumed by tension. Because of this, don't be put off by his initial reactions which may be of resentment or impatience. Massage can be a voyage of discovery, making him easier to ride, less sensitive, and altogether calmer.

For many of us, massage will be just a pleasurable experience, and not necessarily because the horse is not performing to standard. You will gain a deeper understanding of him, and will feel more relaxed and in tune with him as a result.

Today the demand for massage and complementary therapies is growing, largely because many of us don't want to resort to medication and a wait-and-see policy: we prefer massage as a way to prevent more serious problems, and in the maintenance of both our own and our horses' well-being.

What is massage?

Massage can have immediate benefits, but it usually takes regular treatments to bring about significant improvements in health. Initially it provides relief from pain, reduces tension and sedates the nervous system; when the pain has subsided, you can work on correcting the underlying cause of the problems to prevent their return. Healing itself is stimulated by both a mechanical and a reflex action.

The mechanical effect of working on the soft tissues is to relieve tense muscles through relaxation, thereby decreasing pain and increasing mobility, and improving the circulation and lymphatic systems. Reflex action is the involuntary reaction of one part of the body to the stimulation of another part. Because body, mind and emotions work as a whole, connected by energy and the nervous system, touching the skin sends messages to all other parts of the body to reduce the amount of stress hormones – this lowers blood pressure, slows breathing, improves digestion, and generates a sense of well-being. It is believed that massage also helps to release endorphins, the body's natural pain relievers, and to activate neuropeptides, the inter-cellular messages within the nervous system. These link the skin to the nervous system, and the whole body including the immune system, and because of this, massage is thought to have tremendous preventative care benefits.

WHEN TO USE MASSAGE

It is assumed that this treatment will be on a 'normal' horse, meaning one that has not been diagnosed with a veterinary problem. Even so, if your horse is competing, leave at least three clear days between performing this massage and the competition, particularly if it

is your first attempt. Horses are bound to respond differently. Moreover, you will be learning and also developing your own interpretation of the methods that are outlined below and you may need practice in order to establish just how much pressure you need to apply to gain results.

Inevitably your horse will be subjected to many different types of stress in his lifestyle, which can cause postural and gait adaptations. These include the following:

- Horse posture
- Occupational (type of work)
- Mechanical (physical influences such as rider or saddle)
- Traumatic (changes caused by injury)
- Surgical (pre- and post-surgery)
- Disease (changes caused by low-grade disease)

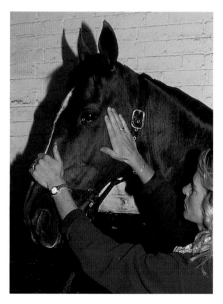

Massage to the head can be used for relaxing the jaw prior to a working session

MASSAGE

POSTURE

A rider can affect the horse's posture and cause certain of the horse's muscle groups to shorten and become tight. Inevitably their opposing muscles – called antagonists – are also affected by reflex inhibition, and as a result weaken. A typical pattern of an incorrectly ridden horse would be of weakened, lengthened abdominal muscles and weak buttock muscles (glutei); in reflex the hip flexors and back extensions become short and tight, then the hamstrings become excessively tight. The muscles eventually adapt to their shortening and the connective tissues lose length and flexibility as well. Of course, if any stress is placed on these weakened and adapted structures, such as galloping from a stand-still or over-exercising in a schooling session, then further damage is done.

Ultimately this muscle imbalance can lead to altered bio-mechanical stresses in joints, causing stiffness or hypermobility.

OCCUPATIONAL

Inevitably a horse will suffer certain stresses as a result of the work he specialises in; potential problems may be, on the one hand, repetitive loading of muscles and joints, and on the other, too limited a range of movement. If he does not use all their available range he will gradually lose the potential to do so. Cross-training will avoid this: for example, a dressage horse might be jumped and galloped in order to utilise the full range of motion of his soft tissue and joints, and so maximise his dressage performance.

MECHANICAL

If your horse has had a musculo-skeletal condition in the past, he may well have developed secondary problems at the time, which have led to postural and gait adaptations. In time these can become primary problems in themselves, due to the changes in

A nice relaxed posture allows normal movement

the soft tissues which lead to unprotected joints and then a painful response.

AFTER SURGERY

If your horse has had surgery, massage may help to maintain mobility; and if he is confined to his box (stall) for a period of rest, or is on restricted exercise, it will help to maintain tone and therefore muscle condition. It also helps psychologically by maintaining contact with you, and it will ease pain and discomfort. And once the surgical condition is resolved, massage is indicated to maintain flexibility of all joints and soft tissues, and to prevent further loss of function.

DISEASE

For horses suffering a permanent low grade disease such as osteo-arthritis, massage pre-exercise will encourage blood flow and nutrition and maintain extensibility. And for those that have suffered foot imbalances which have caused structural changes of the soft tissues, massage helps relax and ease discomfort, and has a significant effect on tension and muscular effort.

MASSAGE

Massage for the Competition Horse

MASSAGE

Massage can be employed during the training of the horse for treatment and rehabilitation, and to enhance athletic performance. It can help to prepare him prior to competition or exercise, and to reduce stress and aid relaxation; and after the effort of hard exercise or competition, it will aid recovery.

At an amateur level, training may sometimes be somewhat neglected, and massage can play a significant role in maintaining tissue pliability and therefore preventing injury. At the other end of the scale, the top equine athlete is more likely to be over-trained, and massage can assist in

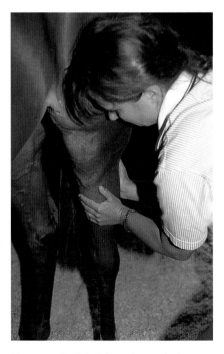

Massage to the limbs helps to improve both co-ordination and power

recovery from fatigue. In this case, two hours should be allowed to elapse before massage is started, for maximum effects; and care must be taken not to go too deep and thereby induce mechanical trauma, and cause detrimental effects on fatigued muscle.

MASSAGE FOR PERFORMANCE

To be able to perform, the body must be able to adapt to the extra stresses placed upon it. The requirements for excellence are power, agility and co-ordination, and in its attainment the horse's body has to cope with activity at the extremes of joint movement and muscle length. This will place heavy demands on the strength and the endurance of the muscle, and the ability of the joints to move freely in all directions; the horse will also need freely mobile connective tissue. Inevitably excess or repetitive stresses, or over-working, will increase the likelihood of other injuries, such as muscle tears. In all cases this results in the connective tissue being replaced by scar tissue, and this will cause a loss of power, flexibility and movement in the tissue; moreover, if the tissue is not rehabilitated before normal full activity is resumed, then it will never re-establish its end limit. This in turn overloads the surrounding tissues, and causes fatigue and over-development of muscle groups.

Massage can be used to stretch and free this inelastic scar tissue – which will have formed restricting adhesions – and return the mobility of the tissue to normal. It will also help to remodel and promote absorption of the scar, and to re-establish full function of the tissues.

Massage can form part of a horse's pre-competition warm up

extreme heat and humidity are examples. This sort of soreness normally sets in after the completion of the event, and sometimes not till the next day. (The less fit animal will also suffer discomfort during such exercise, but as a result of metabolic insufficiency. A well conditioned muscle will not suffer this problem because it has a well functioning capillary bed and a good oxygenated blood supply.) Obviously a horse will be at a disadvantage if he has to carry on competing without having fully recovered from his last efforts – there can potentially be very severe discomfort due to connective tissue inflammation leading to tenderness and stiffness. Massage will delay the onset of soreness and reduce it.

All the scientific evidence strongly indicates that the ideal time to massage is 1–3 hours after exercise in order to enhance athletic performance and for the best therapeutic benefit; also that for certain muscles, massage may have a more lengthening effect than stretching alone.

FATIGUE

When the horse is training very hard he may not recover fully between sessions, and this may lead to general muscle soreness and an increased likelihood of injury. Massage is used to decrease muscle tone and tension, thereby reducing muscular discomfort and promoting relaxation. There is also evidence to suggest that it will help recovery from fatigue, as opposed to rest alone. It would therefore be very appropriate to use it after competitions, training or travelling, or any particularly stressful situation.

MUSCLE SORENESS

Horses suffer soreness in their muscles as a result of extreme exertion and adverse environmental conditions: endurance horses or eventers having to gallop over uneven terrain in wet weather conditions or in

PLANNING A MASSAGE

When planning a massage for a competition animal you should consider at what stage of training the horse is; how fit it is and also the purpose of the massage; this could be:

- to relax
- to tone
- pre-competition to help his warm-up
- inter-competition, to aid recovery from muscle soreness
- post-competition, to improve healing and to prevent adhesion formation
- for general (all over) treatment
- for localised (specific area) treatment
- to relieve acute or chronic injury
- to relieve fatigue/muscle soreness

Preparation

YOUR BODY POSITION AND COMFORT

Doing massage can be quite tiring initially because you are concentrating on a new task and your body is learning new movements, and if you are not careful, this in itself could lead to tension and fatigue. To avoid this occurring, try to work in a systematic way; also, being careful to maintain your own posture and relaxation whilst learning the moves will help to minimise these risks. It is important that the horse feels confident in you, too: as we all know, horses are very good at picking up tension and any lack of confidence; and if you have an injury or potential problem, then it would be as well to consult your specialist to ensure that you are fit to do massage.

Keeping a good posture yourself will mean you are more comfortable and will not fatigue as quickly, and as a result you will enjoy the massage work, and be more relaxed about it, and your horse will pick this up. Altogether this means you will be more effective, and will achieve a better result in massage terms, too.

POSTURE CHECKLIST (1)

- Head up, chin in, look forward.
- Back upright, with relaxed breathing.

- Neck and shoulders loose and elbows flexed.
- Knees slightly bent, feet placed shoulder-width apart.
- Pelvis moves rhythmically; bottom is tucked in.
- Use whole body to transfer energy, *not* just fingertips.

PREPARING TO MASSAGE
Operators

Remove any clothing which may restrict your own movement and inhibit you working hard. Avoid clothes that rustle – for example, some coats and waterproof trousers – as this may cause an edgy horse to become tense. Follow the warm-up exercises described below: these should help prevent fatigue, and help you achieve the results you are striving for in your work. You should be perspiring by the end of a massage if you have been working correctly and have achieved some results.

The Horse

Do not expose him unnecessarily – for instance, if the weather is cold and you are not working on his hindquarters, keep him warm and comfortable. If possible stand him under warm lights **(2)**, though always ensure good headroom. The horse needs to be relaxed, and this is always more easily obtained when not standing on a concrete surface. It is also important for safety.

MASSAGE

Warm-up

Shoulders

- Gently circle shoulders upwards and back, slowly and consistently: x 5 **(1)**.
- Repeat, but go up and forwards with shoulders x 5 **(2)**.
- At the end push shoulders backwards and sustain as if cracking a nut between the shoulder blades: hold for 10 seconds **(3)**.
- Repeat with shoulders hunched forwards, and hold for 10 seconds **(4)**.

Shoulders, Flexors and Extensors

- Let arms hang straight by sides of body. Bring fingers to shoulders and down x 5, both together **(5)**.
- Stand tall and take one arm backwards from side. Do not tilt body forwards. Do one arm at a time, x 5 **(6)**.
- Stand tall and take arm forwards from shoulder; avoid bending backwards. Do one arm at a time. Go as far up to the ceiling as you can **(7)**.

Trunk

- Stand with the feet slightly apart and knees slightly flexed.
- Reach with one hand up and across head to opposite side **(8)**.
- Side-tilt body to this side. Do this x 5, breathing out as you stretch, sliding arm down outside of leg on flexing side.
- Repeat on other side.

Wrists

- Gently circle each way x 3 **(9)**.
- Hold arm extended in front of you: using the opposite hand, sustain wrist extension by applying pressure to front finger tips for 10 seconds. Can be done x 5. Then repeat on the other hand **(10)**.

Hands

- Preparation: rub fingers individually, warming them, and then wring whole hand **(11)**.
- Clench fist, then open hand, repeat x 5 **(12)**.
- Flex middle finger joints and open them **(13)**.

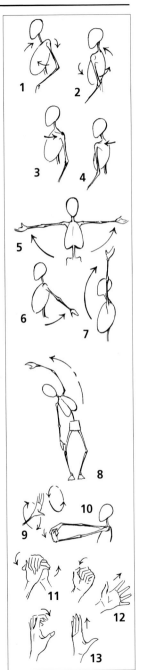

Massage Techniques

Massage involves using a series of movements with your hands which have an effect on the tissues.

STROKING (1)

This is often used initially in a massage and on most areas.

Uses

- To relax the horse.
- To introduce touch.
- To sedate him (slow).
- To stimulate him (brisk).
- To decrease muscle tone (slow)

When to Use

- At the beginning or end of massage.
- When you have only limited time, so on a daily basis.
- To calm and relax him in a stressful situation.

- Any time.

Usually applied from the top of the limb towards the lower end.

Application

- Begin at the beginning or top of the area to be worked.
- Place the whole of your hands in contact with the skin.
- Maintain a *gentle* but firm pressure.

EFFLEURAGE (2)

This is often used on the limbs and when swelling is present.

Uses

- To increase venous and lymphatic return.
- To aid removal of chemical irritants.
- To improve mobility between tissues.
- To stretch muscle fibres.
- To decrease muscle tone.

NOTE: If used *deeply* it can be used to increase muscle tone.

When to Use

- At the start and end of a session, and often in between various techniques.
- Should be performed towards the lymph glands, chiefly located beneath the jaw and throat, near the ear, in front of the shoulder and in the groin.

Application

- Begin at distal part to be effleuraged.
- Make contact with the skin and apply even pressure to sink into the superficial tissues.
- Make a sweeping movement to the top or beginning of the area, moulding to the contours and maintaining the same depth of pressure throughout the stroke.
- Finish the stroke over the lymph gland, then remove the hands and reposition at the start of the next stroke.
- If not to the lymph nodes, continue to the nearest site in that body part.
- Bring your hands towards you as you work, using the heel of your hand.
- Watch that the fingers and palm of the hand don't lose contact.
- Maintain an even depth of pressure while the hands mould to the body contour.
- The following stroke overlaps the first, continuing until the whole of the body region is covered.

NOTE: In a small area use one hand, finger or thumb.

MASSAGE

COMPRESSIONS AND WRINGING

Compressions can be used all over, and are very effective on large muscles. Wringing is often very relaxing; it has a great sedative effect.

Uses

- To aid venous and lymphatic return.
- To help removal of chemical irritants.
- To increase the mobility and length of fibrous tissue.
- To restore mobility between tissue surfaces.
- To aid tissue fluid mobility.
- To increase extensibility and strength of connective tissue.
- Can also trigger skin reflexes and others linked to it.

Features

These techniques compress the soft tissues, then they squeeze or roll them (wringing), working to the tissue end.

When to Use

Use on superficial tissue, ligaments or muscles to soften up large areas.

Application of Compressions

- Use one hand **(3)**, both **(4)**, or pads, fingers, thumbs.
- Begin at the top part and move to end.
- Contact the skin and compress the tissue.
- Skin is moved on the

underlying tissue; there is no glide.

- The hands or digits or back of fist **(5)** are used in a circular motion: this will initiate a slight stretching of the skin behind, and wrinkling ahead.
- If using right and left hand, the right moves clockwise and the left anti-clockwise **(6)**.

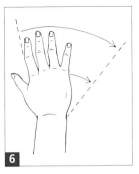

- Pressure is applied to deeper tissues when tissues are compressed. It is a similar movement to opening a child-proof bottle top: press down initially, twisting as you do so, then release (above).
- To go from one completed compression to the next, just slide your hand across.

Wringing (7)

- This requires two hands.
- One hand brings the tissue towards you, the other moves it away. Hold for 2–5 seconds, then release slowly.
- The hands then move to take up position on the adjacent tissue.

MASSAGE

PERCUSSION

Percussion consists of several techniques, the three most important being hacking, clapping and pounding.

Uses

- To stimulate local circulation.
- To provoke muscle and tendon reflexes.
- To provoke a general stimulatory effect.
- To stimulate muscle tone.

Features

Light percussion has an effect on the superficial tissues; heavier application affects deeper layers, and must not be used over the organs.

Application of Hacking (8)

- Hold your arms away from your sides, and flex the elbows to approximately 90° with your wrists fully stretched backwards (extended) and fingers relaxed.
- Your shoulders where possible should be over the area. Stand on something to give yourself the necessary height (see **12**)
- The border of your little finger and hand strike the skin alternately, lightly and rapidly. The movement comes from the wrist, and it involves a full side-to-side movement of the wrist in this position.
- When doing very *light* hacking, only the fingers need strike the skin.

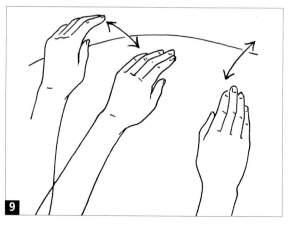

Application of Clapping (9)

- Hold your fingers and thumbs closed together to form a relaxed, cup shape.
- Your elbows should be bent and arms held apart.
- Move one arm and then the other alternately, bending and straightening at the elbow so that the borders of the hands and fingers strike the skin.
- The strokes should be rapid, light and brisk.
- Air is trapped between the hands and the horse's skin and produces a hollow 'clapping' sound as contact is made.

MASSAGE

10

Application of Pounding (10)

- Hold your arms slightly away from your sides, and flex the elbows to 90°.
- Extend wrists and flex fingers loosely into a fist.
- If possible, shoulders should be over the area being treated.
- The outside edge of little finger strikes the skin alternately and rapidly.
- Move at the wrist joint, which moves from side to side.

DIRECT PRESSURE (11 &12)

Uses

To increase circulation by causing an area of vasoconstriction, followed by vasodilation. Spasm is thereby reduced by improving oxygenation of the area.

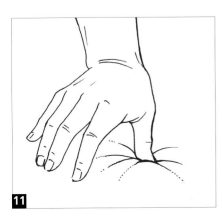

11

Applied Features

To areas of resistance characterised by hardness or sensitivity.
Can be used graded in pressure from light through to heavy.

Application

- Use one or several fingers applied in direct contact to problem areas.
- Use your elbow and bodyweight over the area.
- Use a fist-like grip with pressure directed through the back of the knuckles.
- When applying direct pressure, come off in between light and medium application.

12

MASSAGE

87

CAUTION: Vigorous massage may stress the body in the same way that a training session might, so the horse *must* be allowed a less strenuous routine over the following twenty-four hours. It is not fully known if it is possible to cause significant mechanical trauma to muscles, so take care in the treatment of fatigued muscles.

DO NOT MASSAGE if the horse is suffering from the following conditions:
1 SHOCK (lower blood pressure).
2 FEVER (normal temperature is 38°C/100°F).
3 ACUTE INFLAMMATION (do not address area directly, but it would be acceptable to work elsewhere on body).
4 SKIN PROBLEMS (ringworm).
5 INFECTIOUS DISEASES.
6 ACUTE STAGES OF VIRAL DISEASE (herpes).

SAFETY CONSIDERATIONS WHEN CARRYING OUT MASSAGE (1)
- Perform massage in a box (stall)/stable.
- If there is no handler, tie the horse to single baler twine so that if he pulls away it will break. There needs to be some slack in the rope.
- If a handler is present, always have them stand on the same side as yourself.
- Avoid other animals such as dogs or cats: you want minimum distraction so you can concentrate on the horse, and him on you.
- Keep your free hand resting on the horse, preferably preventing him squashing or kicking you.

- Avoid a situation where you might be trapped between the horse and a wall.
- Use your voice and breathing to help relax and soothe your horse.
- Don't stop working areas of touchiness or sensitivity, just alter the technique: try being more constant in pressure, or resting the hands in a constant hold over the area.
- If you have to use a footstool to stand on, be sure that it is safe in case the horse stands on it.
- Avoid low beams where your horse might hit his head if he reacts by throwing it up.
- Be sure that the horse is standing on a good, non-slip floor.

FURTHER PRECAUTIONS
- If you find hand massage painful, you can use other methods, for example using a mechanical massager. However, many people find that massage loosens and mobilises their hands, especially the less strenuous massage.
- If using lotions/oils, make sure that neither the horse, nor you, has any cuts, as these will sting and cause irritation.
- Always read the label. Check that any lotion/oil is safe to massage, and that it is not just to be applied lightly – otherwise you may cause blistering.
  - Always do a skin test with massage oils both on the horse and on yourself first.
  - Check for allergies and prohibitive substances.
  - Try to prevent the horse pulling back.
  - Provide a good, non-slip surface for the horse to stand on.

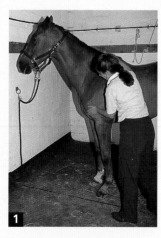

MASSAGE

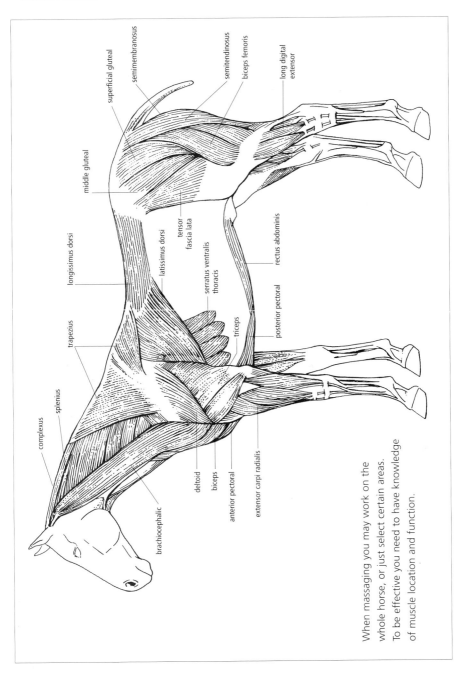

When massaging you may work on the whole horse, or just select certain areas. To be effective you need to have knowledge of muscle location and function.

Labels: semimembranosus, superficial gluteal, semitendinosus, biceps femoris, long digital extensor, middle gluteal, longissimus dorsi, tensor fascia lata, latissimus dorsi, serratus ventralis thoracis, rectus abdominis, trapezius, triceps, posterior pectoral, splenius, complexus, deltoid, biceps, anterior pectoral, extensor carpi radialis, brachiocephalic

The Neck

MASSAGE

TOP LINE OF NECK

Step 1: Start with stroking from top of neck towards withers **(1)**. Do x 1 light, x 1 medium, x 1 heavy.

Step 2: Then do neck wringing along the line of mane from poll to withers **(2)**.

Step 3: Follow up with compressions using one hand. Start from base and work towards ears. Do x 1 light. Then repeat medium pressure, and finally x 1 heavy **(3)**.

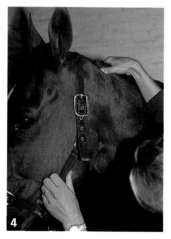

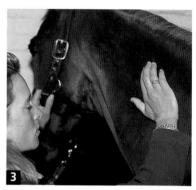

UPPER NECK

Step 1: 2cm (¾in) behind atlas apply pressure using thumb **(4)**. Use light for 20 secs, followed by medium for 15 secs and, if tolerated, heavy for a further 15 secs. In between each grade of pressure, lighten and then reapply medium pressure and so on.

Step 2: Apply medium compressions to area to finish off **(5)**.

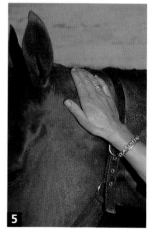

 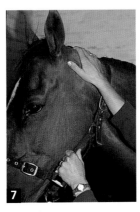

MUSCLES: UNDERSIDE OF NECK
BRACHIOCEPHALICUS

Step 1: Slide up from base of neck towards poll using one hand in an effleurage movement **(8)**.

Step 2: Do light pressure x 2, and then medium pressure x 2, keeping hand in contact as you return from finish to start position. Move slowly and carefully. Note any areas of sensitivity.

Step 3: If sensitive areas still present by completion of strokes, using thumb apply direct pressure for light 20 secs and then a further 20 secs at medium pressure.

Step 4: Follow up with compressions to whole muscle.

ATLAS

Step 1: Using whole hand or thumb, slide up from wing of atlas to poll, just behind ears, mimicking a rubbing action **(6)**. Go up and down light, and then up and down medium.

Step 2: Watch for reactions. If sensitive or sore apply a constant application of light pressure for 20 secs, followed by medium for 20 secs **(7)**. Lighten pressure between each grade of pressure application, and then reapply.

Step 3: Follow up with compressions using single hand to site of application of direct pressure. Use light, followed by medium.

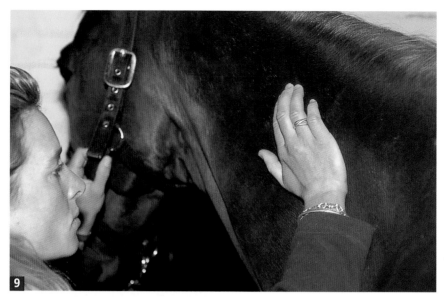

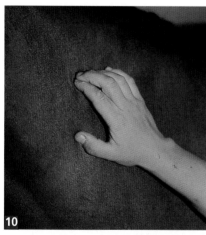

MUSCLE: SPLENIUS

Step 1: Apply compressions along the middle of the neck from base to ears. Apply light pressure twice, and then medium pressure twice to entire length **(9)**.

Step 2: Zigzag palpation or line palpation to detect resistance or sensitivity in tissue **(10)**.

Step 3: If detected, then apply direct pressure using thumb or back of fist **(11)**. Use 20 secs light pressure, followed by 20 secs medium pressure. Come off in between each grade of pressure and reapply.

Step 4: To close, use compressions along the length of the muscle at medium pressure **(9)**.

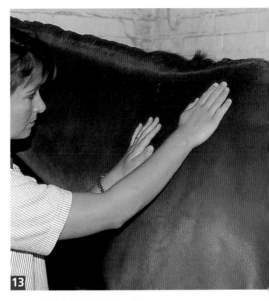

BASE OF NECK AREA

Step 1: Use a stroking action with the left hand working from the withers down in front of the shoulder at base of neck; the right hand rests on the shoulder **(12)**. Apply using light pressure, and then at medium pressure. Do entire area twice with each pressure.

Step 2: Use palpation techniques, thumb or fingers, to identify areas of sensitivity **(13)**.

Step 3: If positive, then apply direct pressure with left hand over the area, using elbow, back of hand or fingers **(14)**. Apply light pressure for 20 secs, come off, and reapply at medium pressure for 20 secs. Then lighten contact before reapplying at deep pressure for 10 secs.

Step 4: Finish off with compressions to the entire area at medium pressure.

MASSAGE

93

Withers

MASSAGE

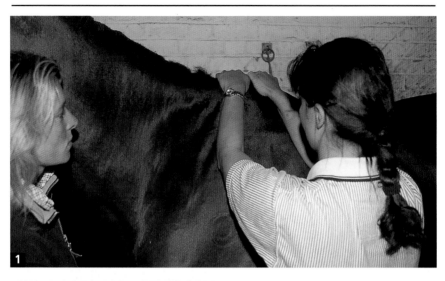

THORACIC TRAPEZIUS

Step 1: Start with a modified wringing technique. Bring the withers slowly across with both hands towards you, hold and push across to other side. Do whole section, moving along as you go **(1)**.

Step 2: Clapping: using one hand, in handshake position apply to soft tissues along line of withers and behind scapula **(2)**. Use light pressure and avoid any bone. Work over area back and forth three times.

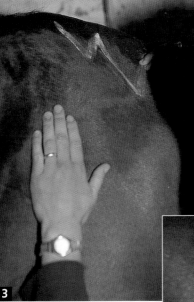

Step 3: Zigzag palpation: apply to area to identify reactions or muscle spasms **(3)**.

Step 4: If reactive, apply direct pressure using thumb or two fingers **(4)**: use light pressure for 20 secs, then medium pressure for 20 secs.

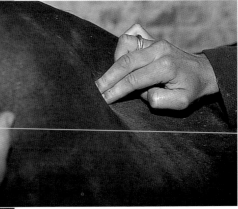

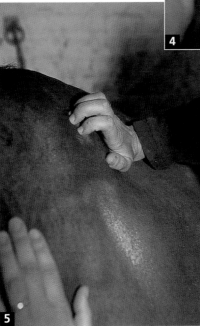

When on left side, use your right hand to stroke tissues from head to tail direction. Do the entire area twice for the three different pressures. Lighten, and reapply at medium pressure for 20 secs.

Step 5: Follow up with compressions, single-handed, to whole area **(5)**.

Shoulders

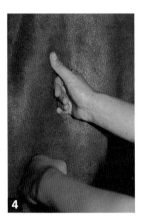

MUSCLE: DELTOID

Step 1: Using the stroking technique, work down the shoulder to the top of leg three times at light pressure, and then three times at medium pressure. From the side, this is the section of the shoulder nearest the head **(1)**.

Step 2: Compressions single-handed from top to bottom, using light pressure once and medium pressure once to entire area **(2)**.

Step 3: Finger palpation to identify muscle spasms or sensitivity **(3)**.

Step 4: If present, apply direct pressure to the area using back of hand **(4)**: do at light pressure for 20 secs, and then lighten and reapply at medium pressure for 20 secs.

Step 5: Finish off with medium pressure compressions, single- or double-handed, along muscle length **(5)**.

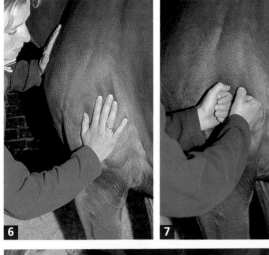

TRICEPS

Step 1: Use two hands to cover the area at the middle and back of the shoulder, or divide into two areas: stroke from top to bottom twice at light pressure, then twice at medium pressure, and twice at heavy pressure **(6)**.

Step 2: Backhand compressions from bottom of area to top at medium pressure, covering each area twice **(7)**.

Step 3: Hacking: apply to whole area at light pressure going from top to bottom, and back up again, twice to each section; then repeat at medium pressure **(8)**.

Step 4: Palpation using thumb or two-finger line technique to identify resistance or sensitivity **(9).**

Step 5: If sensitive or tight, apply direct pressure with fingers or back of hand **(10)**. Use light pressure for 20 secs, then lighten and reapply at medium pressure for 20 secs, followed by 20 secs at heavy.

Step 6: Complete with single-handed compressions at medium pressure, up down twice **(11)**.

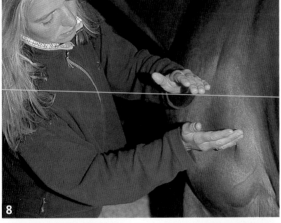

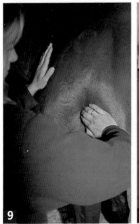

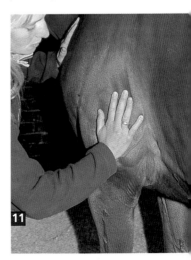

MASSAGE

Chest and Front of Shoulder

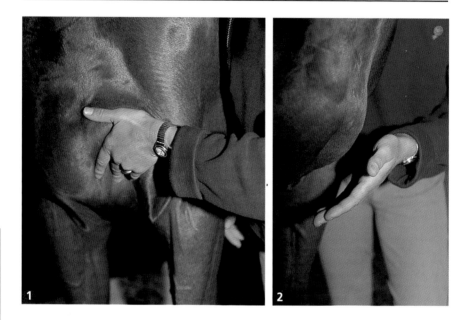

BICEPS AND ANTERIOR PECTORALS

Step 1: Stroking **(1)**: Cover the area using medium pressure strokes. Repeat twice.

Step 2: Clapping **(2)**: Use one hand and apply at light pressure twice, and then medium pressure twice, to whole area.

Step 3: Palpation **(3)**: Using fingers or cat's paw, palpate to detect muscle spasm or resistance.

Step 4: If positive, apply direct pressure using two fingers or back of hand **(4)**, at light pressure for 10 secs, then medium pressure for 20 secs, and finally heavy pressure for 20 secs. Remember to lighten in between each pressure change.

Step 5: Finish with clapping single-handed **(2)** at medium pressure twice over the area.

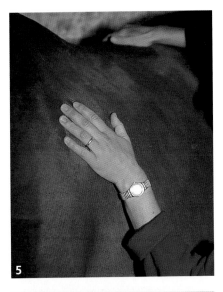

SERRATUS THORACIS

Step 1: Stroking **(5)**: Apply light pressure twice to each area, and then medium pressure twice to the area from the top and back of the shoulder blade and across the chest wall.

Step 2: Clapping **(6)**: To the whole area at light pressure twice, followed by medium pressure twice.

Step 3: Finger palpation to identify any areas of irritability or spasm **(7)**.

Step 4: Direct pressure to area if positive **(8)**: Start light for 20 secs, then lighten and reapply at medium pressure for 20 secs.

Step 5: Compressions: Single-handed across area and length of muscle at medium pressure twice **(9)**.

MASSAGE

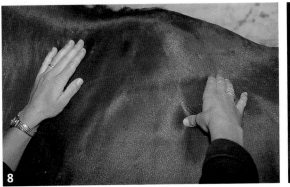

Girth Area

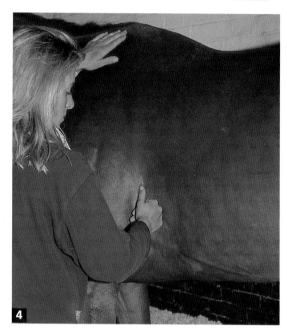

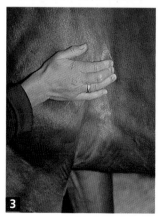

Step 1: Stroking: From half way down ribcage to stomach – do in several divisions if necessary – at medium pressure **(1)**. Go down and repeat several times.

Step 2: Compressions **(2)**: To whole area at medium pressure three times.

Step 3: Two-finger palpation to identify problem areas **(3)**.

Step 4: Direct pressure to area of reaction using light pressure for 20 secs, then lighten and reapply at medium pressure 20 secs. Use thumb or back of hand technique **(4)**.

Step 5: Apply compressions to the area treated with medium pressure **(5)**.

MASSAGE

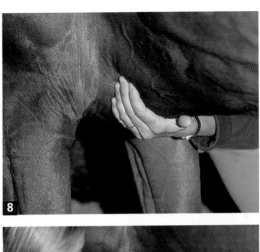

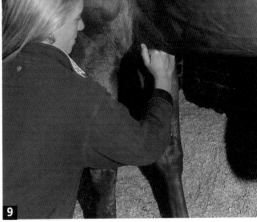

POSTERIOR PECTORAL

Step 1: Stroking: From front of horse to back, using light pressure and then medium pressure **(6)**. Do entire area at each pressure twice.

Step 2: Clapping with one hand at light pressure twice, and then medium pressure twice **(7)**.

Step 3: Cat's paw for palpation to detect problem areas. Do from opposite side of horse and bring across to midline **(8)**.

Step 4: If a problem area is detected, apply direct pressure using your thumb for 20 secs at a light pressure, then lighten and reapply at a medium pressure for a further 20 secs **(9)**.

Step 5: Use single-handed compression to area treated at a medium pressure. Apply over area three times.

Foreleg

EXTENSOR CARPI RADIALIS

Step 1: Stroking all down the leg using two hands at a light pressure twice, followed by medium pressure twice **(1)**.

Step 2: Effleurage from the base of the leg up to the elbow: cover all the leg using two hands in sections **(2)**. Do light pressure twice, followed by medium pressure twice to whole area.

Step 3: Compressions from above the knee to the top of leg at medium pressure twice. From the left side of the horse, place right hand on the back of the upper leg, and use your left hand to apply the compression technique with one hand to the front of the leg **(3)**.

Step 4: Finish with stroking from the top of the leg down the front and side. Apply twice at a medium pressure **(as 1)**.

MASSAGE

102

Back

LATISSIMUS DORSI/ LONGISSIMUS DORSI

Step 1: Stroking along the area using a light pressure, then medium pressure **(1)**. Do twice along for each.

Step 2: Hacking along the area at light pressure, and then at medium pressure twice along **(2)**.

Step 3: Palpation **(3)**: Work with thumb and index finger on either side of spine, and run along muscles on either side of spine. Identify reactive areas. Do this with light pressure initially, and then a medium pressure.

Step 4: Apply direct pressure to any area of spasm using two fingers at light pressure for 20 secs, then come off and reapply at medium pressure for a further 20 secs **(4)**.

Step 5: Compressions along length of muscle at medium pressure **(5)**. Go along entire area three times.

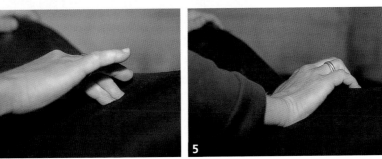

MASSAGE

Abdomen

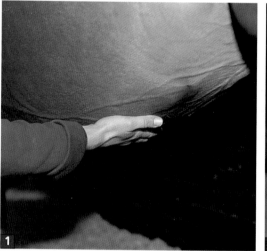

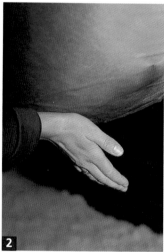

RECTUS ABDOMINIS

Step 1: Stroking at medium pressure, three times along area of muscle **(1)**.

Step 2: Clapping **(2)** using light pressure three times to the area.

Step 3: Apply the cat's paw palpation to identify spasm and to initiate a belly lift: use two hands, and apply from opposite side under stomach through to your side **(3)**; apply lift using medium pressure with finger tips. Observe top of back for small amount of lift. The horse may resent this, so take care and keep an eye on his hind limbs and teeth! Apply along area several times.

The horse should drop his head as he lifts his back.

Step 4: Hacking at light pressure to area. Go up and down three times.

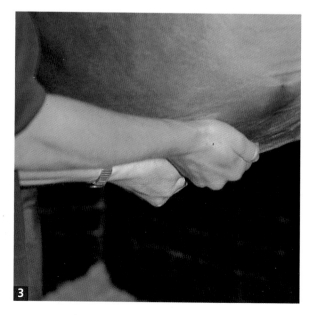

Hindquarters

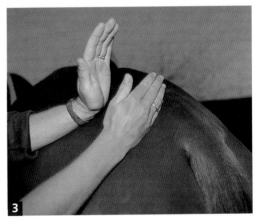

MASSAGE

GLUTEI (BUTTOCKS)

Step 1: Stroking **(1)**: Divide the area into sections (see diagram page 30). Do at light pressure along it several times, then at medium pressure.

Step 2: Pounding **(2)**: Divide into sections. Go up and down area three times, then repeat at medium pressure three times.

Step 3: Hacking **(3)**: Divide into sections, and go up and down three times at light, and then at medium pressure.

Step 4: Zigzag palpation through each section **(4)** to detect areas of resistance and irritability.

Step 5: If positive, apply direct pressure using the back of your hand, thumb, two fingers or elbow **(5)** – light pressure for 20 secs, then medium for 20 secs and heavy for 20 secs over the area of resistance. Come off in between each grade of pressure, then reapply to the next level.

Step 6: Compressions at medium pressure, covering the whole area and surround, up and down three times **(6)**.

Step 7: To close, clapping to the whole of the glutei in sections **(7)**. Cover the area at least three times at medium pressure.

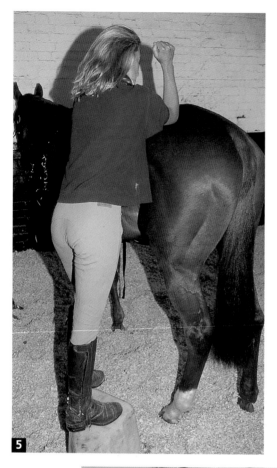

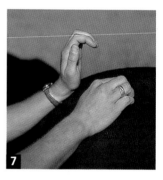

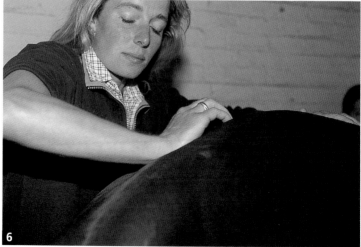

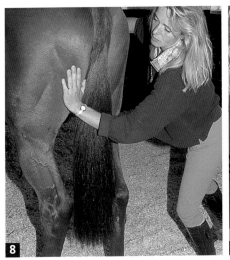

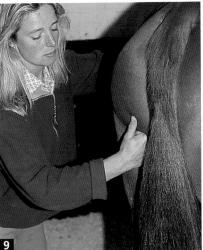

SEMI-MEMBRANOSUS (HAMSTRINGS)

If your horse is touchy, you can reach from the opposite side and across to this area.

Step 1: Stroking: Apply from top of rump down outside of limb **(8)**. Cover area at light, and then at medium pressure several times.

Step 2: Compressions: Apply single back of hand to length of muscle **(9)**. Go up and down at medium pressure twice.

Step 3: Cat's paw palpation: To identify areas of resistance in the muscle. Do down the whole length of the muscle **(10)**.

Step 4: Apply direct pressure to areas of muscle spasm, using back of fist or thumb **(11)**. Use light, then medium, and finally heavy pressure at 20 secs each. Lighten and reapply in between each grade of pressure.

Step 5: Compressions are used to finish the area **(12)**; work along the whole of the muscle belly, twice at medium, and then twice at heavy pressure.

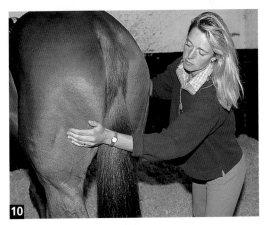

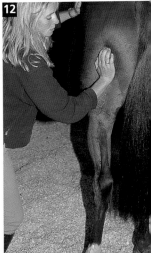

SEMITENDINOSUS (HAMSTRINGS)

Step 1: Stroking: Apply from seat bone down across side of quarter **(13)**. Apply to whole area at light pressure twice, and then at medium pressure twice.

Step 2: Compressions: Double back-handed along length of muscle **(14)** at medium pressure, covering area twice.

Step 3: Palpate: Line palpate to identify resistant or sore areas.

Step 4: Direct pressure: Apply to sore/tight areas at light pressure for 20 secs, then at medium pressure for 20 secs, followed by heavy pressure for 20 secs. Lighten and reapply in between each level of pressure **(15)**.

Step 5: Compressions: Apply along length of muscle up and down twice at medium pressure, and then at heavy pressure **(16)**.

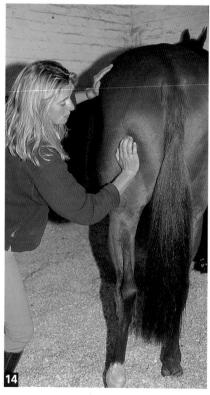

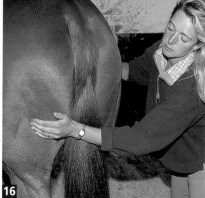

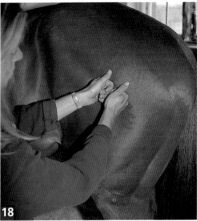

BICEPS FEMORIS (HAMSTRINGS)

Step 1: Stroking: Apply from middle of quarter across to stifle **(17)** at medium pressure twice, followed by heavy pressure twice.

Step 2: Compressions: Use double back-handed technique **(18)** and divide into two divisions. Start at top and work down, at medium pressure. Do each division two times.

Step 3: Palpate with fingers **(19)** to identify resistance.

Step 4: Direct pressure: Using back of hand **(20)**, apply light pressure for 20 secs, then medium pressure for 20 secs, followed by heavy pressure for 20 secs. Come off in between each, and reapply.

Step 5: Compressions to finish off, using double-handed technique **(as 18)** at medium pressure, and heavy pressure to length of muscle. Do whole area twice.

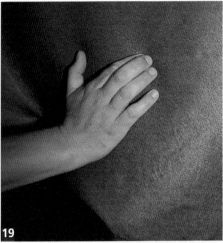

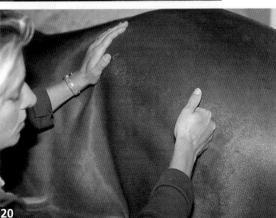

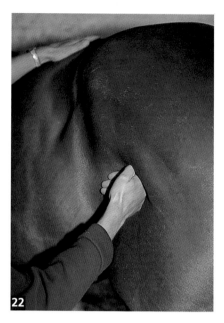

TENSOR FASCIA LATA

NOTE: Can be a sensitive area, so take care.

Step 1: Stroking: Apply from tubercoxae down towards stifle area **(21)**. Apply at medium pressure. Repeat twice.

Step 2: Single-handed compressions from bottom to top of the area **(22)**, at light and then at medium pressure. Do whole area twice for each.

Step 3: Finger palpate for sensitivity or resistance **(23)**.

Step 4: Direct pressure is then applied to any areas of problem, using 20 secs light, then 20 secs of medium pressure, with fingers or back of hand **(24)**; lighten in between each grade of pressure.

Step 5: Compressions to finish **(as 22)**, at light pressure and then at medium pressure. Do whole area twice.

Hind leg

LONG DIGITAL EXTENSOR

Step 1: Stroking down the whole leg, using two hands – divide the limb into areas. Repeat at light pressure x 2, and the same for medium **(1)**.

Step 2: Effleurage from the bottom of the leg to the top at light pressure, and then medium pressure twice **(2)**.

Step 3: Compressions to top half of leg from hock up, using single hand. Left hand applies compression to front of limb, and right hand supports back of upper limb area. Apply light pressure twice, and then lighten and follow up with medium pressure. Do the whole area twice for both **(3)**.

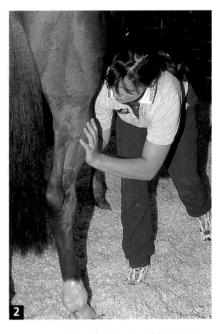

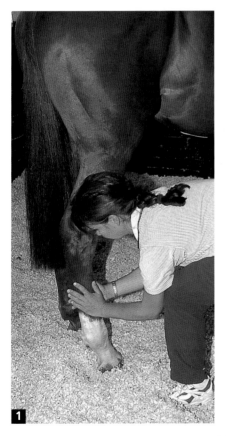

MASSAGE

IMPORTANT INFORMATION ON THE USE OF MASSAGE

MASSAGE DOS AND DON'TS

- If massaging only one area of the horse before exercise, follow up with suppling exercises for that area also. Once the horse is warmed up – after 20 minutes of exercise – then the stretching exercises can be performed to the whole horse, or one specific area.
- After a massage it is a good idea to walk the horse in hand, to ease him off, and also to offer fresh water to drink.
- When applying massage 1–3 hours post exercise, do not do any of the direct pressure techniques, and only apply light and medium pressures in the other massage techniques.
- If the horse is suffering acute muscle pain or spasm from recent injury, avoid massaging directly to the affected areas, but apply massage in the surrounding areas. This will help resolution of oedema and in maintaining nutrition to the muscles.

HOW OFTEN TO MASSAGE

- In theory, a normal horse could have a full body massage as described daily.
- If, on palpation, you discover he has areas that require direct pressure techniques, then he may need to have some exercise modifications.
- If you find points of reactivity in the withers or girth or back areas *ie* where direct contact with tack or rider will be made, and you apply direct pressure to them, the horse should be rested from tack for that day. He may be exercised in other ways where no contact from tack or rider is made.
- If you wish to ride or compete on that day, *avoid* direct pressure techniques, but apply the rest of the massage programme as outlined.
- If you do not have much time, ten minutes spent on the hindquarters would give the most benefit before exercise.

WHEN MASSAGE IS NOT PRODUCTIVE

- If you continue to get areas of irritability, sensitivity, muscle spasm or resistance, please refer to a professional, preferably your veterinary surgeon, to eliminate other primary sources of discomfort.
- If you find that, despite applying the direct pressure technique, the areas of sensitivity remain, then again you may need to enrol the help of a physical therapist, once cleared by your vet, to mobilise the area initially.

MASSAGE

The terrain poses hidden stresses on the front legs, as shown here

Exercise Therapy

The aim of this chapter is to identify the most beneficial approach to exercise in the context of suppling and stretching therapy, and how to progress from beginning to end. Many injuries are caused because the horse's body is not adequately prepared for the demands placed upon it, and because we have changed his management and lifestyle to such an extent. It is therefore important for our horses that we work out a programme of injury prevention and maintenance of function based on an understanding of progressive exercise. The middle section of this chapter provides a full and comprehensive regime of suppling and stretching exercises, from exercises that can be performed by yourself on a horse that is doing very little exercise, to a horse performing a full stretching and ridden exercise programme. It is hoped that following such a regime will serve as the best possible preparation the horse can have for the job he has to do.

The last section considers alternative methods of exercise: some of these are used as part of the warm-up and warm-down stages, some are an important part of the exercise programme itself. They include lungeing, long-reining, use of the round pen and/or the horse walker, swimming and treadmills.

Supplying Exercises

There are two categories of supplying exercise: one is the passive application of supplying exercises administered to the horse by yourself before he leaves the box or field for exercise; these can be performed after a massage programme and after exercise as well. The other is dynamic supplying, exercises that are performed when the horse is under saddle or being driven, and as part of the warm-up and warm-down periods.

PASSIVE SUPPLING EXERCISES

These are employed to warm up the tissues and joints, to loosen them up and prepare them for exercise **(1)**. They can be done on a cold horse because we are not holding the end of range and therefore not applying a continual stretch on the tissue. They are performed on the head and neck, forelimbs and shoulders, and hindquarters and hind legs. They are carried out slowly and within the comfort of the horse. Wherever possible

make him move about quietly first – perhaps around the yard – because this will make your work easier.

DYNAMIC SUPPLING

Here the joints are put through their full range of movement actively, by muscular contraction and weight-bearing, as in locomotion. Such exercises are very beneficial for scapula mobility and for flexibility of the spinal column. The sort of exercises might be large circles progressing to smaller ones, and lateral movements; also work over poles **(2)**,

and on gradients – up and down hills. These employ active limb flexion and extension through a wide range of movement.

The effect of passive and dynamic supplying exercises is to improve the horse's overall performance by improving the quality of the movement produced. Thus the horse will be better protected against injury, and will be able to react readily to adverse external stimuli.

STRETCHING

Joints and tissues must not be stretched when they are cold, nor when there is an acute injury. The effects on the musculo-skeletal system are to create permanent lengthening of the structures. A slow, low force as applied in stretching takes time to have effect, but the results are long term, remaining even after the force has been removed.

Stretching the tissues and therefore increasing their range of movement also enhances the speed with which they can adapt, and therefore their shock absorption ability. This all decreases injury risk. The effect of slow stretching after a work-out is to decrease the risk of post-exercise muscular soreness; also, because the tissues are thoroughly warmed up, there is maximum potential for increasing extensibility.

EXERCISE THERAPY

EXERCISE THERAPY

The practical incorporation of passive and dynamic suppling and stretching into a progressively structured exercise regime should be considered in three main parts: the warm-up, the exercise itself, and the warm-down.

The Warm-Up

This is the period of adjustment from rest to exercise when exercises are performed before activity. These are designed to improve performance and to reduce the chances of injury by mobilising the horse mentally and physically, by using all the major muscle groups in a controlled, rhythmical way. In effect the warm-up will serve to increase:

- body and tissue temperature;
- blood flow through active muscles;
- heart rate;
- metabolic rate;
- oxygen utilisation;
- the speed at which nerve impulses travel, helping the body movements;
- physical work capacity;
- the muscles' ability to relax and contract faster and more efficiently.

It will also help to decrease muscular tension.

The warm-up should prepare the horse's body for its specific activity. It should also prepare the joints by working them through their normal range of movement. Moreover the tissue fibres around the joints are lubricated by synovial fluid warmed within the joint. All the major joints should be mobilised.

The next stage is the pulse raiser, which aims to increase the temperature and blood saturation of muscles and tissues, preparing them to accept stretching with minimum risk of injury. This starts with slow, low-impact movement at walking pace and builds up to larger, controlled movements which will raise the pulse rate into the lower end of the training zone.

The next phase is ideally the stretching zone, when all major groups should be

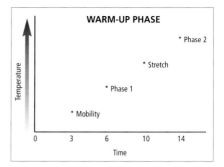

stretched: this *must* be done properly to have a positive effect.

The last phase is the vigorous mobility stage, when further increases in heart rate and respiration are achieved, to pre-vigorous exercise performance level. Also longer and faster body movements are carried out. It is important that the deep muscle temperature is raised, because then the tissues will be more pliable, minimising the likelihood of any resistance. This allows muscles to contract with great speed, off-setting the risk of injury.

The warm-up is related to the main part of the exercise session in so far as it is rehearsing and utilising the movement patterns necessary for the horse's particular discipline. Note that in warm climates the body warms up more quickly, and therefore less time is required.

Uphill work is good for cardio-vascular fitness and improving flexibility of muscles. This range of movement would encourage full extension of the hind limbs and stretch of spine muscles

115

The Warm-Down

This is just as important as the warm-up phase. It should be more progressive, and gently decrease the exercise, but should resemble the warm-up in activity. It is very important to perform stretches on completion of exercise to prevent soreness and stiffness; this helps to maintain good balanced muscle tone and therefore function, which in the longer term gives better quality of movement and posture.

THE PRACTICAL EFFECTS OF STRETCHING AND SUPPLING

Stretching and suppling exercises have many beneficial effects:

- They will encourage relaxation and decrease muscle tension; they will also improve the circulation, and increase the extensibility of muscles and tendons, ligaments and capsules. This will help prevent areas of hyper-irritability and decreased oxygen (trigger points) forming.
- They will increase the flexibility and range of movement of the joints, and improve the horse's co-ordination, meaning that he will be able to adapt to, and so cope more readily with, any extreme forces and stresses placed upon him.
- They will help to improve his muscle fibre tone and so his length of stride and general elasticity, thereby enhancing his ability to control his speed of movement.
- All of the above physical improvements will help his mental attitude, improving his own self-confidence and ability to think for himself.

GUIDELINES FOR THE PRACTICAL APPLICATION OF STRETCHING

Stretching exercises should only be administered when the tissues are warm: after massage; after the warm-up stage of an exercise routine, ie 10–20 minutes exercise; at the end of the 'warm-down' phase.

- The limb or joint is held at the end of the range of movement available for 10 secs, or until it relaxes. Then ask for more stretch, and hold for 10–20 secs. Never bounce. Always release slowly, and return to start position.
- When stretching and suppling, always support the limb with two hands, one above and one below the joint. Apply any force with the upper hand, and guide with the lower hand.
- Warning: if at risk of being stretched too far, the muscle will spontaneously contract in self-preservation. Watch for this and stop: it is most important never to fight or stretch the horse too far.
- Don't start stretching old stiff joints with a known problem: work above the joint and below, and seek advice.
- Don't stretch areas where there has been acute muscle damage.

PRACTICAL TIPS FOR YOU AND YOUR HORSE

For You

- Breathe out at the point of maximum effort.
- Ensure a good base of support and good balance.
- Keep your body, and especially your hands and arms, relaxed and mobile to follow the movement.
- Try and observe a good posture:
    chin tucked in
    tall head on neck
    straight back
    bottom tucked in
    feet firmly on floor.
- Never allow your back to support the weight of the horse, but always lift using your legs, and with pelvis and lower abdominal muscles supported.
- Place your elbow supporting the horse's weight onto your knee for extra support.

For Your Horse

- Make sure he is standing attentively and prepared, *ie* four square for balance.
- A helper should hold on the same side as yourself.
- To persuade the horse to pick up a forelimb, if he is refusing to do so, apply gentle pressure behind the knee at the top of the cannon and push him over gently; with a

hind limb, apply pressure below the hock and push him gently over.

- Allow enough room to perform movements.
- Only work on a good, non-slip floor.

ADAPTED SUPPLING REGIME

If for some reason you cannot perform the suppling and stretching exercises safely, then there are alternative ways that you can exercise the horse to achieve the results you want. The following exercises can be done in hand, when long-reining, or on the lunge:

1 Walk over poles placed flat on the ground: do this three times **(3)**.

2 To progress, raise one end and walk over the poles; do this on both reins.

3 Form a star with the poles resting on a bale or small block. Vary the height to increase the difficulty, from low becoming higher. Walk the horse over the widest part of the star, and then move towards the centre. Do this on both reins.

4 Make a maze with poles on the ground, and walk the horse through it; increase the difficulty by narrowing the width and

PRACTICAL APPLICATION

Suppling exercises can be carried out in many circumstances, including the following:

- Before exercise.
- After massage.
- At the end of an exercise session as a modification of a stretching programme.
- Before turnout/lungeing/ swimming.
- With any horse – young or old, fit or unfit.

Its main uses are to promote mobility, increase circulation and prepare the body for exercise. When you embark on a suppling or stretching session, remember the following:

- Loosen the horse's rugs (blankets) to allow ease of movement.
- Do easy movements or limbs first if he resents any area being done.

increasing the bend. Do this on both reins.

5 Rein back three steps on the level. Progress to six steps. Remember always to walk the horse forwards afterwards.

6 To increase the exercise difficulty, rein back up a slight incline, then progressively increase the incline and the number of steps. (Never pull on the horse's head, but teach him to go back from the chest.)

7 In hand, ask the horse to move sideways by crossing his hind legs and taking his weight across. Do this both ways.

8 Do small 5m circles, making the horse go forwards. All of these exercises can be done by anyone on any horse that is *allowed to move*.

9 Do all these exercises three times a week for maintenance; they may be done before exercise.

10 If you are not able to perform acomplete massage, simply employ your hands to groom with. Use stroking movements.

The Forelimb

EXERCISE THERAPY

A suppling exercise regime is an integral part of preparing the horse for any physical exertion, and for maintaining him in good health. It can be done with any horse, young or old, fit or unfit.

When to do:
- Before exercise
- After massage
- Before turnout/lungeing/swimming
- At the end of an exercise session as a modification of a stretching programme

Uses:
- To promote mobility
- To increase circulation
- To prepare for exercise

EXERCISE 1: PASTERN FLEXIBILITY

Step 1: Left hand supports the back of pastern, with the thumb along the line of the pastern **(1)**. The rest of your hand encircles the base of the fetlock and front of pastern. The right hand is on the toe.

Step 2: Flex the toe towards the fetlock **(1)**, and then gently away to start position **(2)**. Repeat in total x 3.

EXERCISE 2: SHOULDER AND FORELIMB FLEXIBILITY

Step 1: Pick up the foot as if you were going to pick it out. The left hand supports the inside of the cannon bone halfway down; the right hand supports the front of the lower part of the pastern and hoof wall **(3)**.

Step 2: In this position describe a clockwise circular movement with the toe of the foot **(4)**. Do this slowly and in a small movement to start with, and progress to larger circles for increasing mobility as it becomes easier to do. Do each way x 3.

Note: The movement should be a perfect circle and feel easy to perform; if restricted it will feel jammed at a certain point. Go the easy way first, and then re-attempt the tighter movement to see if it has improved.

TIP: You can rest yourself and the horse in between each exercise, or just continue into the next one straightaway.

5

6

Step 3: Describe circles performing movement forwards, and circle back to the beginning. Do clockwise and anti-clockwise. Repeat x 3.

8

EXERCISE 3: ADDUCTION
Step 1: Start position as for exercise 2.
Step 2: This time bring the limb across towards the opposite foreleg and perform circles as you take up this position **(5)**. Work clockwise and anti-clockwise slowly in small circles.
Note: Keep limb low to the ground.
Step 3: Continue circular motion and go back to start position. Repeat x 3.

EXERCISE 4: ABDUCTION
Step 1: As for position in exercise 2.
Step 2: Bring leg away from body, guiding with left and right hand. Keep leg low to the ground **(6)**.
Step 3: Describe small circles clockwise and then anti-clockwise, performing the movement away from side. Progress to larger ones

when comfortable. Do each way x 3.

EXERCISE 5: PROTRACTION
Step 1: Start position as for exercise 2.
Step 2: Move left hand to support back of knee. Bring limb forwards in advance of opposite leg **(7)**.

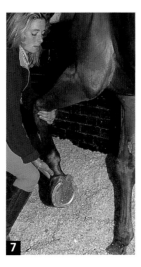

7

EXERCISE 6: RETRACTION
Step 1: Left hand rests over the front of the knee. Right hand applies support around pastern below fetlock **(8)**.
Step 2: Standing facing your horse's shoulder with feet well apart, transfer your weight from your left to your right foot.
Step 3: Describe circles with whole leg from the shoulder through to the knee and foot as you move limb backwards and then forwards again. Repeat x 3, alternating clockwise and anti-clockwise.
Note: Remember to keep limb low to the ground.

Further Exercises for the Forelimb

These supling exercises carry on from the ones just described, but are performed with more clearance of the ground and with greater knee flexion and more emphasis on the shoulder movements.

Tip: Do not hold at the end of the range, or go too far. This is not a stretching exercise, it is just a loosening exercise.

EXERCISE 1: GENERAL LOOSEN-UP

Step 1: Hold the knee in a flexed position with the right hand supporting the inside of the fetlock, and the left hand on the inside of the knee area and just below it. Have your body facing the horse, with his limb resting against your thighs **(1)**.

Step 2: Describe a circular movement each way, in small and large circles. Use your bodyweight and arm position to direct the movement; go anti-clockwise and clockwise.

Step 3: At the end of the movement progress straightaway to the next position, or allow a rest before doing so.

EXERCISE 2: ADDUCTION

Step 1: Rest the left hand on the inside of the limb above the knee – it provides support and produces the direction of movement. The right hand provides support on the outside of the fetlock and pastern.

Step 2: Guide the limb across the front of the horse's chest, performing circles with the knee as you go. Do not go very far: this is *not* a stretch.

Step 3: Return to the start position, performing circles both ways as you go.

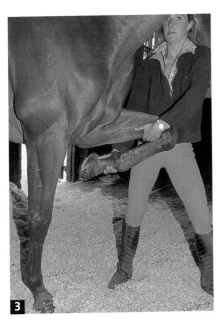

3

EXERCISE 3: ABDUCTION

Step 1: One hand supports the inside of the fetlock **(1)**, and the other the top of the cannon bone: then come over the top of the limb to take up position. Support the limb with your thighs, with flexed knees and a good stance. Alternatively place the left hand on the inside and top of the foreleg, sliding it into the armpit area, then bring the leg out sideways from here in a circular movement.

Step 2: Describe a circular motion from your hips and pelvis, keeping the horse's limb with you. Gently encourage the circles out and away from the horse's body. Repeat three times each way: the circles may be small to begin with, then progress to larger ones as the horse relaxes.

EXERCISE 4: PROTRACTION

Step 1: The left hand provides support inside and just below the knee, with the right hand over the top of the fetlock joint **(3)**.

Step 2: Transfer your weight from your right to your left foot, and bring the limb forwards performing circles as you go, with the knee describing the circles. Move slowly and in both directions.

Step 3: Return to the start position and repeat, describing circles the opposite way.

EXERCISE 5: RETRACTION

Step 1: Rest the left hand on the front of the knee; the right hand provides support below the fetlock and over the pastern **(4)**.

Step 2: Transfer your bodyweight from the left to the right leg, describing circular movements as you do so clockwise and then anti-clockwise, taking the leg backwards from the neck.

Step 3: Return the limb to the ground carefully: *do not let it drop.*

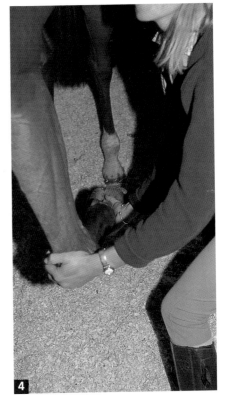

4

EXERCISE 6: ELEVATION AND DEPRESSION

Note that this exercise does not go very far, and the horse may be put off balance.

Step 1: Flex the horse's knee: support the leg with both hands, one over the inside of the knee and the other round the fetlock. Position your body close up against the horse, thighs supporting his leg **(5)**.

Step 2: Fix your eyes on top of the scapula. Lift the limb and shoulder blade slowly upwards towards the sky, then lower it slowly **(6)**.

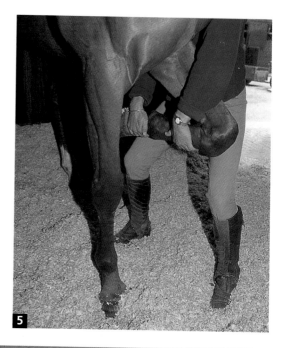

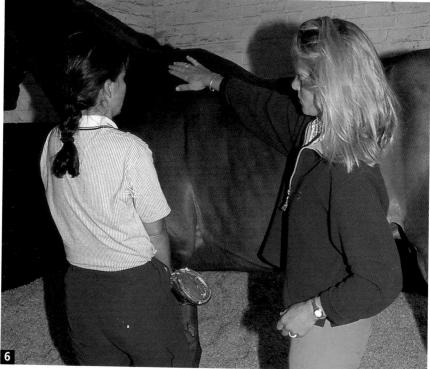

122

The Hind Leg

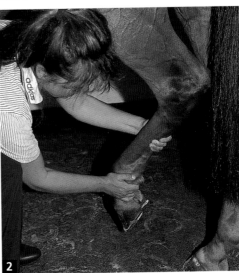

EXERCISE 1: GENERAL MOBILITY

Step 1: Pick the foot up as if to pick it out. Hold it just above the ground with your left hand around the front of the fetlock and your right hand around the back of the cannon bone just below the hock **(1)**.

Step 2: Describe small circles slowly anti-clockwise x 3, then clockwise x 3.

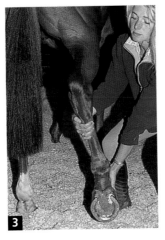

EXERCISE 2: ADDUCTION

Step 1: Take the limb slowly across to the opposite limb, performing circles anti-clockwise and then clockwise as you go **(2)**.

Step 2: Go slowly, making the circles small, then progressively larger. Do x 3 each way.

EXERCISE 3: ABDUCTION

Step 1: Take the limb out to the side **(3)** without throwing the horse off balance, performing circles as you go.

Step 2: Perform slow circles anti-clockwise and clockwise, and return to the start position in the same way. Do x 3 each way.

When performing suppling exercises to the hind leg, be sure that you observe the following safety measures:

- Check that your horse is standing four square and is attentive.
- Ensure that you are bending your knees.
- Keep your back as straight as possible at all times.
- Maintain a good base of support.
- Remember to breathe out on effort, and to use your whole body to produce the movement.

EXERCISE 4: FLEXION/PROTRACTION

Step 1: Take the limb, still keeping close to the ground, forwards towards the front leg, describing circles anti-clockwise and clockwise as you go **(4)**.
Step 2: Do small and large circles slowly. Use circles to go back to the start position.

EXERCISE 5: EXTENSION/RETRACTION

Step 1: Take the leg backwards, performing circular movements clockwise and then anti-clockwise as you go **(5)**.
Step 2: Keep the circles small to begin with, gradually progressing to larger ones, and working slowly.
Step 3: Work your way back to the start position, performing circles as you go.

THE HIND LEG: LEVEL 2

Exercises 1–5 can be done with the leg higher off the ground, therefore asking greater flexion of the hock: follow the steps exactly as in 1–5 above, but with this new leg position **(6)**.

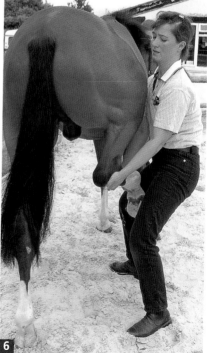

124

The Tail

Take care when performing these suppling exercises because the horse may resent his tail being handled. If this is the case, only use the following exercises after massage to the glutei: this should relax the area and allow you to progress to these exercises with less risk to your own safety.

EXERCISE 1

Step 1: Stand to one side to assess in relative safety the horse's response to your handling his tail. Standing on the horse's right side, the left hand holds the tail firmly one-third of the way down, whilst the right hand supports the top of the tail from underneath **(1)**.

Step 2: Gently lift the tail away from the rump and circle it slowly clockwise and anti-clockwise; do this x 3 each way.

Step 3: Return the tail to its resting position, fully supporting it all the way.

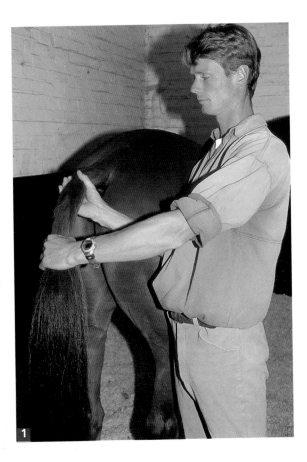

EXERCISE THERAPY

Stretching Exercises

These exercises, and stretching of any sort, should only be performed …
- once the horse has really warmed up;
- after massage;
- after 10–20 minutes of exercise;
- at the end of an exercise session.

Stretching brings the following benefits:

- It improves the range of the joints and soft tissues permanently.
- It improves the co-ordination, and prepares the body for work.
- It prevents injuries.

All the examples here are described as from the left side. Once you have completed one area, do the opposite side *ie* do the left shoulder, and then the right.

Warning: Do not stretch in acute muscle pain or spasm.

Remember: to lift with your upper legs and buttock muscles, whilst keeping the lower back straight. Your knees should be slightly flexed.

The Neck

Study the pictures carefully so you do these exercises properly. For instance, there is a right way and a wrong way to stretch the horse's upper neck muscles: **(1)** shows how not to do it – note the head tilt, and observe that the nostrils are not level – while picture **(2)** shows the correct way. You may need to use a carrot initially to teach your horse to do these exercises.

EXERCISE 1: NECK

Step 1: For stretching the upper neck area, place horse against a wall with his bottom in the corner to prevent trick movements.

Step 2: Place your back and shoulders against the horse's neck near the head, blocking the rest of the neck area **(3)**; *or*, using your hand against his face, block the movement with your right hand whilst the left hand rests over the front of his head, gently encouraging him to turn to your side.

Step 3: Ask the horse to rotate his head around to the same side as you. Keep his nostrils level, and do not let him side-tilt his head or neck as he comes round. Use your hands to assist and prevent trick movements. Hold for 10 secs if possible.

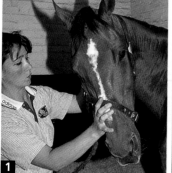
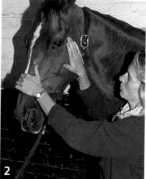
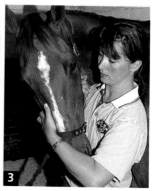

EXERCISE 2: MID-NECK

Step 1: Place your body in the middle part of the horse's neck space and into his shoulder. This encourages more bend in the upper and middle neck area.

Step 2: Ask in the same way as exercise 1 for him to come round.

Step 3: Hold for 10 secs.

EXERCISE 3: LOWER NECK

Step 1: Move along to the lower part of the neck and encourage rotation from the top, all down the neck to the side **(4)**.

Step 2: Place your back and shoulders against the horse's neck near the base; or, using your hand against his face, block the movement with your right hand whilst the left hand rests over the front of his head, gently encouraging him to turn to your side (4).

Step 3: Ask the horse to rotate his head round to the same side as you. Keep his nostrils level, and do not let him side-tilt his head or neck as he comes round. Use your hands to assist and prevent trick movements. Hold for 10 secs if possible.

EXERCISE 4: NECK EXTENSION

Step 1: This can also be done using a stable door, or a chain across the door. Varying the height of the obstacle will encourage different ranges of extension **(5)**.

Step 2: Stand on one side with the horse up against the object, and offer him an incentive to encourage him to lengthen his neck and tip his head back to extend it **(6)**.

4

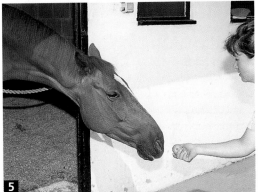

5

6

EXERCISE 5: NECK FLEXION

Step 1: Position the horse against the wall, with his backside in the corner.

Step 2: Offer an incentive, or encourage him to nod his head towards his throat **(7)**.

Step 3: Then encourage him to move his muzzle towards the front of his chest **(8)**. Try to sustain this position for 10 secs.

Step 4: Encourage him to move his muzzle towards his knees, or to the floor between his front legs **(9)**.

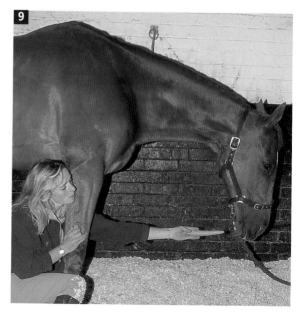

Forelimb Stretches

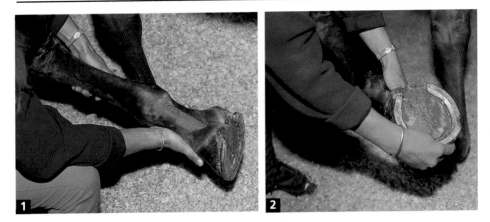

EXERCISE 1: THE FETLOCK

Step 1: Support the inside of the cannon bone with the left hand; the right hand holds the front of the hoof **(1)**.

Step 2: Bring the bulbs of the heels up and back towards the fetlock joint **(2)**.

Step 3: At end of the movement, hold the position for 10 secs.

Step 4: Slowly unwind the flexed position out to full extension. Hold for 10 secs, and repeat three times.

EXERCISE 2: KNEE FLEXION

Step 1: Rest the left hand on the inside of the lower leg just below the knee. Do not go over the top, do it from the inside, or you will obstruct the knee bend. Place the right hand on the outside of the pastern **(3)**.

Step 2: Take the lower half of the leg up towards the elbow.

Go slowly, and take care not to bruise the elbow with the shoe.

Step 3: Hold this end position for 10 secs, then ask for a little more bend at the knee, trying to make sure there is no daylight between the lower leg and the upper leg. Hold for a further 5 secs.

Step 4: Replace the lower leg slowly to an almost straight position, then repeat back into flexion. Repeat in total three times.

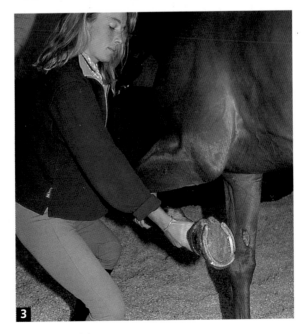

129

Shoulder Stretching

EXERCISE 1: EXTENSION/ PROTRACTION

Step 1: Stand facing your horse and flex his knee, the right hand supporting just below the fetlock, the left hand resting inside the limb **(1)** below the knee. Transfer your weight from your right to your left foot, and guide the limb forwards towards the horse's nose – apply a sustained stretch: hold for 10 secs **(2)**.

Step 2: Ask for further stretch, and hold for a further 5–10 secs.

Step 3: Return the leg to the start position, so it is in line with the opposite limb, and allow the horse to rest. Repeat three times.

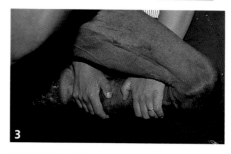

EXERCISE 2: ABDUCTION

Step 1: Flex the knee, then stand facing the horse's shoulder, supporting the limb against the thighs with both hands on the inside of the lower limb **(3)**.

Step 2: Transfer your bodyweight backwards, bringing the limb with you.

Alternative position for steps 1 and 2:

Place the right hand up into the chest area alongside the attachment of the forelimb to the body **(4)**. As you move your weight, use your left hand to bring the limb with you, so the soft tissues from limb and chest are together.

Step 3: Hold this position for 10 secs, then apply more stretch and hold a further 5–10 secs.

Step 4: Slowly release back to the body. If the horse needs to rest, replace the limb to ground, and repeat from beginning. Repeat in total three times.

EXERCISE 3: SHOULDER EXTENSION

Be careful the horse does not collapse or over-stretch. *Keep the limb in line with the horse's body* – do not pull it out **(5)**.

Step 1: Place your right hand behind the horse's knee, the left hand supporting the lower limb around or behind the fetlock. Keep your eyes

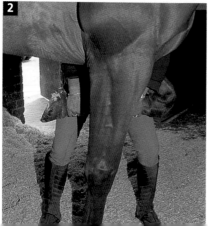

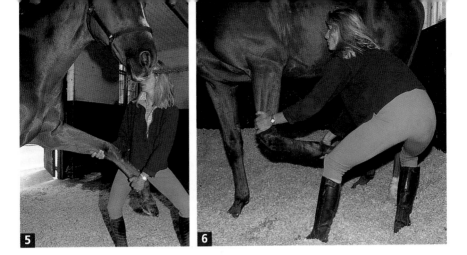

focused along the shoulder and into the wither and back area.

Step 2: Transfer your weight sideways to your left foot, whilst at the same time your left hand guides the lower limb out to the extended position. Your right hand supports, guides and applies the stretch to the upper limb **(5)**.

Step 3: Maintain this position – with the limb almost fully straight at the knee – if possible for 10 secs; then ask with the right hand for a little more stretch for a further 5–10 secs.

Step 4: Bend the knee and return off stretch. If your horse is comfortable, do it again. Repeat three times at most.

EXERCISE 4: SHOULDER FLEXION/RETRACTION

Be careful when doing this stretch – always go slowly, and don't expect too much movement. Go as far as is comfortable for the horse, and watch for signs of resistance – he may try to pull the limb upwards.

Step 1: Place the left hand above the knee on top of the limb. The right hand supports the fetlock and pastern on the inside.

Step 2: Focus your eyes on the lower neck and shoulder, and ask

for backward movements by transferring your weight from your left to your right foot **(6)**.

Step 3: Hold this stretched position for 10 secs. Then apply slightly more stretch for 5–10 secs by using your left hand.

Step 4: Relax the left hand, and return the limb to the start position, so that it is in line with the opposite limb. Repeat three times in total.

EXERCISE 5: ADDUCTION

Avoid excessive twisting on the limb, and ensure that the whole leg moves across.

Step 1: The right hand holds the fetlock/pastern; the left hand supports the outside knee and cannon.

Step 2: Take the flexed limb forwards towards the horse's nose, then using the left hand, apply pressure across the outside of the limb to meet the opposite foreleg **(7)**.

Step 3: Hold this position for 10 secs, then gently apply a further stretch for 5–10 secs. Return to start position.

Step 4: Take up limb from position back in line with opposite leg, and reapply stretch position and stretch to the limb. Repeat three times in total.

Hind Leg Stretches

EXERCISE 1:
HOCK FLEXION
Step 1: Stand at the rear of the horse facing his hip, and place your feet fairly far apart for maximum support: then pick up your horse's leg. Support it with both hands between the hock and the fetlock **(1)**.

Step 2: Raise the leg upwards as in a flexion test. Do not push the horse over. Relax at the end of the movement, and let the horse relax down into your hold.

Step 3: Hold for 10 secs, then flex a little more and hold for a further 5 secs.

Step 4: Replace to the ground for a rest, or progress to the next exercise.

EXERCISE 2:
PROTRACTION
Step 1: As for step 1 of exercise 1; then take the limb forwards towards the fetlock of the front leg – keep it low to the ground as you do so **(2)**.

Step 2: At the point of resistance stop, and hold in a relaxed position to a count of 10 secs.

Step 3: At the end of 10 secs ask for a little more stretch, and hold for a further 5 secs.

Step 4: Slowly unwind, back to the beginning. Repeat x 3.

Step 5: If happy, carry on to the next exercise.

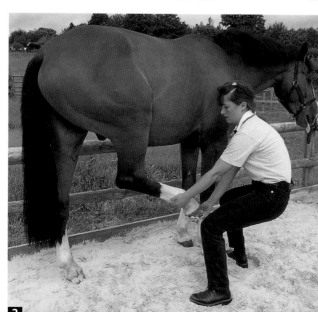

WATCHPOINT:
By asking for the stretch with your hand on the toe you are increasing the tension. Some horses may find this difficult, so instead put both hands on the fetlock.
If the horse reacts suddenly you may injure your hand.

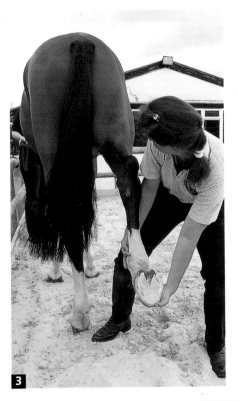

EXERCISE 3: RETRACTION

Step 1: Stand at the thigh of the horse, facing his rear. Place your feet apart, one in front of the other.

Step 2: Pick up the horse's foot as if you were going to pick it out. Support the leg with your inside hand over the top of the hock or on the 'inside of the area below the hock, and the lower leg with your outside hand across the front of the hoof or fetlock **(3)**.

Step 3: Slowly bring the leg backwards keeping the foot pointing downwards, long and low to the ground, extending the fetlock. When resistance is felt, hold for 10 secs, then ask for a little more stretch for a further 5 secs.

Step 4: Slowly unwind back to the beginning, and repeat. Do x 3 in total.

EXERCISE 4: ADDUCTION

Step 1: Bring the leg from the opposite side across and under, aiming for the opposite hind leg and just in front of it **(4)**.

Step 2: Hold on for 10 secs, then ask for a little more, holding for a further 5–10 secs, then return to the beginning.

EXERCISE THERAPY

Tail Stretch

If your horse is sensitive around the tail, always do suppling exercises first. If he does not become more relaxed, back him up to the door and position yourself on the other side (instead of standing directly behind him or to one side). Do this for all the exercises on the tail area. Be careful as you release the stretch, because sometimes the horse may kick out.

EXERCISE 1

Step 1: The left hand guides the tail up and out **(1)**.

Step 2: The right hand supports and applies the stretch at the top of the tail; hold for 10 secs, then relax off slowly.

Step 3: Maintain contact, and bring the tail slowly round to the horse's side **(2)**.

Step 4: Apply a gentle stretch; the horse's body should remain still, and should *not* side-tilt. Hold for 10 secs, then gently let off, and return tail to neutral start position.

Step 5: Repeat to the opposite side, as above.

Step 6: The right hand supports the tail, and lifts upwards, whilst the left hand moves towards the rump, forming a question-mark shape with the tail. Hold for 10 secs, then slowly release **(3)**.

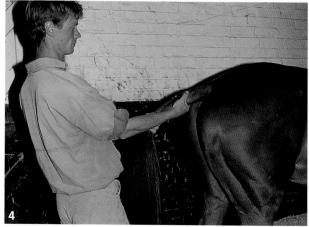

Step 7: Hold the tail as in **(3)**. Position yourself with one leg in front of the other, and gently take up the tail slack, transferring your bodyweight from the front to the back foot **(4)**. Feel the take-up of slack of the tissues from the tail through to the neck. Hold for 10 secs, and *very* slowly release. Support the tail down to its resting position.

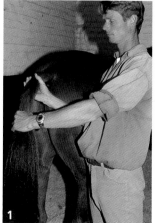

Alternative Methods of Exercise

LUNGEING

Lungeing is one of several alternative methods of exercising; others are long-reining, the round pen and the horse walker. Some are used as part of the warm-up and warm-down; some are the mainstay of the exercise programme itself. To avoid injury and to increase flexibility, suppling and stretching exercises should be done alongside any other form of exercise. Lungeing is beneficial in the following ways:

- It teaches a horse to go forwards and to accept verbal commands;
- It can help train the rider whilst they are on the horse;
- It can be used to warm up a horse prior to exercise;
- The horse can be exercised without the encumbrance and pressure of the rider's weight;
- It develops control and the horse's muscle development, therefore improving his flexibility and co-ordination.

It is important not to over-lunge by fixing the horse in his way of going and thereby fatiguing him. To be lunged

on a tight circle requires considerable athleticism and a good level of fitness on the horse's part: a more positive way of producing good movement and balance is to use two lines. This requires a degree of competency and skill, but it allows greater control of the shoulders and hindquarters, and so encourages a more correct movement. Using more space in the school prevents

continual torsional strain and encourages more forward movement; this may also allow a gentler progression to true lungeing.

Horses should warm up and down on the lunge just as in ridden exercise. Thus when asking for more roundness and collection, the horse should also be given time to soften and relax, and he should be allowed to stretch down in between exercises. It is important to consider what equipment to lunge in: for example, your horse may perform better in a lungeing cavesson (1) than in a bridle; he might prefer the lunge line connected to the bridle and not over the poll; or the lunge lines themselves may be too heavy. Experiment with different attachments and weights of line to see what suits him best (2).

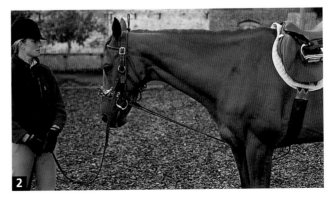

head posture. Always make the horse step forwards immediately afterwards. Be sure the movement is not rushed. If he needs encouragement, this should be a touch on the chest or limbs. This exercise promotes engagement of the hindquarters and use of the stomach muscles to create spinal flexion and therefore elevation of the withers

Be sure that there is no pressure on the spine from roller or saddle, also that it is placed correctly. It is very important to allow freedom of elbow and chest wall muscles. If too far forwards the roller or saddle can also cause pressure on the shoulder blades and inhibit their movement.

Lastly, lungeing on a good, non-slip surface, hard or soft, is one way to evaluate the horse's soundness.

EXERCISES ON THE LUNGE

- For unbalanced, weak horses, use large circles **(3)** and frequent changes of direction. Never work them for too long, and build up the work gradually.
- Progress to lungeing on a 20m circle on a mild incline: this improves the integration of the muscles and awareness, and also the response mechanism of the body.
- Frequent transitions will help to improve balance, but they must be smooth, with the horse maintaining a natural posture and balance. When halting, the movement must come from the hindquarters, with good spinal flexion.
- Exercises should include backing up (also done in hand) on the flat, and when competent, up an incline. The horse should halt, then go back one or two strides whilst maintaining his balance and with a correct

and then a normal head and neck position. Progress to strike-off into canter from halt with the horse maintaining a good balance.

- Counter canter can be used to strengthen the back muscles, but must only be performed once the back has been reasonably developed.
- Work over ground poles encourages spinal/hindquarter flexibility, but never use too many **(4)**. Introduce two or three at a time keeping them flat on the ground to begin with, and raising them first at one end and then at both. Such work helps develop abdominal lift and good back posture.

NOTE: Some surfaces are very deep and may produce excessive strain on an unfit horse, so use them carefully. Always use the best possible surface, one that is even and with good shock-absorption capabilities. Avoid a deep, heavy surface that might well risk a strain.

5 **6**

LONG-REINING

Uses two lines, and useful in several ways:

- Working the horse in straight lines is less stressful to his limbs than on a circle **(5)**.
- Teaching movements that will be performed ridden, particularly lateral work **(6)**.
- For starting young horses **(6)** as it teaches them to go forwards, and the directional aids (left and right).
- For any horse that is weak or needs help learning straightness, because it promotes symmetrical muscle development.
- For teaching driving horses to flex and use their shoulders correctly.

Long-reining offers much greater freedom than lungeing because the horse can be worked wherever you like – all over the school and out in the country. He can be made to perform all the school movements on long-reins – circles, serpentines, loops – as big or as small as you like, according to his stage of training, with the advantage that the two lines encourage better engagement than would be possible just lungeing. Basic long-reining can be done on different surfaces and gradients to encourage fuller development and better movement of the body. Always start on the level, and introduce hills and moving across gradients as fitness improves. Long-reining in and out of obstacles and over ground-poles **(7)** will also improve his co-ordination, flexibility, and muscle strength.

Driving horses can suffer stiffness if they have not been trained or ridden under saddle, and long-reining can introduce to their training regime flexibility exercises that are not possible just on the lunge or when driving. Horses that are only driven should be long-reined regularly to teach and maintain correct movement and flexibility.

As in all things, if you are not experienced at long-reining and feel you need help, do not hesitate to seek professional advice.

7

8

initiated by Monty Roberts. The advantage of the round pen in training is that the horse is completely free, and therefore only submits to his handler when he feels he is ready: in the long term this means that his whole attitude is more trusting and willing, without the resentment or fear that is often present if he is *made* to submit.

Another advantage is that the horse can discover his own balance, and can be worked on both reins without the restraints

THE ROUND PEN

The method of training based on the use of the round pen **(8)** is becoming increasingly popular. The round pen itself has several uses:

- To loose school the horse.
- To establish a good relationship with the handler, whereby the horse submits freely.
- To allow the horse that has suffered injury, free but restricted exercise.
- To break in, or reback a horse using the training method known as 'join-up', as

imposed by a rider. This is particularly helpful for young horses in the first stages of breaking in and training, for older horses suffering a back problem, and for horses with a rider-induced problem, such as bridle-lame, resisting and pulling, leaning on the bit, altered gait.

As in all schooling, however, be careful not to overdo exercise sessions on a circle, as this can cause undue stress on the joints. Furthermore, too small a circle can be

9

detrimental to balance, and again can cause enormous stress to the limbs.

It is always advisable to walk the horse in hand and do suppling exercises before working in any loose school.

Finally, the quality of the surface in the round pen – or any school, come to that – must be good otherwise the horse risks hurting himself, and will certainly lost confidence.

HORSE WALKER

Most large and busy yards (farms) now have a horse walker **(9)**, and consider it invaluable, for several reasons:

- It eases the horse into work at the beginning of his season.
- It prevents boredom if the horse is stabled all the time.
- It helps the body's circulation and prevents stiffness on a day off.
- It is useful as a warm-up and warm-down pre- and post-exercise.
- For gait re-education using weighted boots.

The horse walker is essentially a labour-saving device, as up to six or eight horses can be exercised at once, with only one person in surveillance. Horses are moved on a circle at a controlled and regulated speed, and the walker can be made to go in either direction on the circle.

As always, however, there are things to watch out for: too much of this exercise could unduly stress horses with old joint problems; the surface must be secure and of good quality if horses are not to risk slipping; and the horses' attitude must be constantly monitored. For example, if a horse is lazy and stops using his back end, he could well trip and risk injury; and if he suddenly panics he could be at risk – so watch that his posture is relaxed and correct.

SWIMMING

Swimming pools **(10)** for fitness or remedial training in horses are generally circular or straight in shape. They are used a lot in racing as a warm-up, or if for some reason the horse cannot continue with his normal fitness programme. They are not normally heated. Horses can also be swum in the sea, or in natural ponds or lakes.

Some horses like swimming and swim well, others do not. To swim well the horse must use his back and limbs evenly – if his hindquarters keep sinking, or if he keeps twisting and turning on his side, then he is not a good swimmer. Swimming is not valuable as a training device in the long term as it is no

substitute for cardiovascular training, and does not encourage correct muscle development (since the posture of the horse is opposite to what it is when he is ridden). It does, however, bring certain benefits:

- It is useful post surgically for some lower joint problems to aid movement and circulation.
- To rest the limbs from the concussive effects of weight-bearing exercise.
- To rest the horse from fast work but maintain a certain fitness.
- To aid circulation and reduce swelling.
- Psychologically it helps horses to relax, and staves off boredom.

Straight pools are better for the horse

because they cause less strain on his frame, and he finds it easier to keep his balance. In a circular pool there should be a handler on each side of the horse so that the pull on the headcollar is even, first so that it doesn't unbalance him, and also to encourage him to use his back and limbs evenly.

Swimming is no substitute for normal work, however, mainly because it does not sufficiently prepare the cardiovascular system for the fast work required in so many competitive events.

TREADMILLS

Treadmills can be a permanent fixture, or they can be hired for a short period of time. There are now water treadmills, too, though here we shall only look briefly at ordinary treadmills. They can be beneficial in the following ways:

- When the horse needs to rest his back from the weight of a rider due to injury.
- For warming up or down.
- As a substitute for hill work.

- For gait re-education – the horse can be fitted with weighted boots.

Treadmills are normally used on a flat or inclined plane, with one horse at a time. The horse can walk forwards to come off, or go backwards if the treadmill is fixed. They are used for scientific purposes, to monitor the horse's heart rate and breathing, and to measure body fluids. They are also used to give the horse walking and trotting exercise when he first comes out, and if he is too excitable to ride on the roads.

The floor of a treadmill must be carefully maintained, so there is no alteration in the horse's gait.

It is also important that the horse's head carriage is steady and in the correct position: this will help keep him straight on the treadmill.

Warning: The effect of continual usage of the treadmill should be considered, as the moving forwards of the hind leg by the treadmill is not a normal movement.

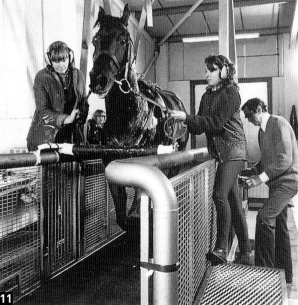

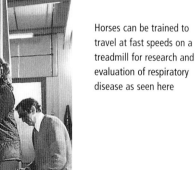

Horses can be trained to travel at fast speeds on a treadmill for research and evaluation of respiratory disease as seen here

Training Aids/Devices

The use of so-called training aids to help develop and produce normal movement can be a controversial issue. When they are used by experienced professionals who understand their effect, and can assess how appropriate they would be, they can be helpful in certain instances. Problems arise when those who are perhaps less knowledgeable use them without understanding their action: then their benefit is limited, indeed they often have a positively detrimental effect on the horse's movement, and sometimes even create a physical problem. It is important always to assess your horse's problem and eliminate all the potential reasons why he is unable to perform correctly before using a training aid. For example, if your horse will not accept the bit it is essential to double check the following possible problem areas before you resort to using schooling aids:

• teeth • saddle • rider
• Pain somewhere?

If he feels pain or discomfort in any of these areas, he is unlikely to give a settled, obedient ride. If, however, there are no problems here, and you have applied the correct ridden and training methods, then when used under the guidance of your trainer, these training aids may help to resolve some of the issues. So, when you have fitted your chosen device, be critical of your horse's movement as he is working, and ask yourself if you are really achieving what you set out to do. Observe his flexibility and gait pattern, and assess its fluidity and normality

of movement. By asking one part of the horse to do something, are you in fact restricting it and failing to achieve and/or maintain full function throughout his skeletal frame?

A common fault is for the training aid to cause the horse to become stilted and on the forehand, with consequent loss of suppleness through his back, and equally loss of engagement of his hindquarters. Used incorrectly, it will oblige the horse to work with his body in an unnatural posture for an extended period of time; like this he will tire quickly and will then compensate by using other parts of his body incorrectly – and in these circumstances he will be much more susceptible to incurring injury.

Of the many training aids available, we will consider just three: side-reins, the Chambon, and drawreins, as probably the ones in most common use.

Side-reins (1) are used to help teach the horse to accept a rein contact, and sometimes to help provide control. They must be fitted to allow for the horse's natural carriage, outline and movement; they should never be fitted so tightly that they pull his head in, thereby restricting his movement.

1 = DIRECTION OF MOVEMENT

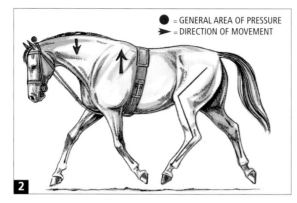

= GENERAL AREA OF PRESSURE
= DIRECTION OF MOVEMENT

2

The Chambon (2) should only be used when the horse is on the lunge. Its purpose is to encourage the horse to stretch his neck down, and work with a rounded back and engaged hocks.

Drawreins (3&4): With drawreins there is always a risk that the horse will be pulled onto his forehand and become stilted in his movement. Used correctly, the horse will be encouraged forwards, and guided with a light, sympathetic hand so that he works actively through his whole body, with a lower head carriage and in a rounder shape.

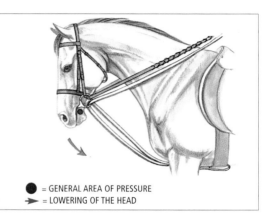

= GENERAL AREA OF PRESSURE
= LOWERING OF THE HEAD

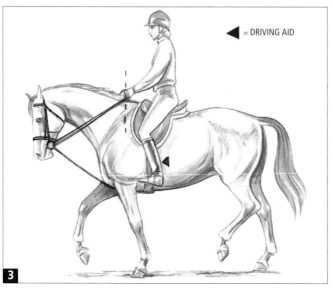

= DRIVING AID

3

142

Specific Regimes for Specialist Disciplines

This chapter takes a closer look at some more specialised areas of equestrianism, and the demands that each discipline places upon the horses operating within it. The whole approach of this book so far can be applied to any horse, at any stage of its training; however, specialist disciplines often require a sports-specific approach. There is tremendous growth in some of these areas, and the horses are better helped by more specific regimes in order to prevent problems, particularly if, as owners, we are not very experienced. Finally we look at a regime for our old and faithful friend retired at grass. At some point we will have to acknowledge that his quality of life has deteriorated to an unacceptable level, but until then we can help keep him supple and comfortable for as long as possible. Furthermore, loneliness and boredom often go hand in hand with advancing years, and can often lead to depression and a rapid deterioration in condition and mobility; so daily contact (or whenever you can) through massage and suppling exercise can be enormously beneficial for both of you.

Endurance Riding

The ideal type of horse for endurance competitions is between 15hh and 16hh with a naturally lean, athletic build, typically an Arab or an Arab cross. It must have strength combined with speed and stamina, and due to the intense nature of the demands of fitness it must stay sound and cope with a variety of terrains, so strong healthy feet are imperative. In some climates the endurance horse will experience intense humidity and heat, so it must be able to dissipate heat and cope with it. Endurance riding is a fast-growing sport, and one of the few where health, condition and fitness are judged throughout and are an integral part of the competition, with veterinary inspections before, and at set points during and after it.

TRAINING

The training for a 100-mile ride takes at least three years, with slow steady work to increase strength and stamina; the regime would also include strength training, dressage movements, and suppling and stretching exercises.

Strength training develops the propulsive power in the hindquarters, so the horse can tackle steeper gradients. Working up and down hills of increasing steepness plays a large part in this, as does the number of times the climb is repeated.

Ridden dressage movements help to maintain the horse's suppleness, and therefore soundness, by increasing the capability of all his joints to absorb concussion. Also, because he must round his back and use his hindquarters as he engages, so his propulsive forces and flexibility are improved, which in turn will help him cope with hills and difficult terrain. The dressage movements should include turns, circles and lateral movements.

Suppling and stretching exercises, and massage, are all very good for relieving tension and post-exercise soreness.

MANAGEMENT AND CARE

Diet and training must be carefully worked out, and closely monitored, if muscular problems from dehydration and electrolyte imbalances are to be avoided. Fatigue is caused by overheating, incorrect diet, and as a result of this, glycogen depletion; and exhaustion will result if the horse suffers dehydration, and if his temperature and his respiration rate go unacceptably high. Initially he will show muscle cramping symptoms manifested in gait abnormalities which might range from mild to severe.

Well fitting, suitable tack is of paramount importance. In particular an endurance horse has to wear his saddle for long periods of time, and so it is essential that it fits appropriately. Be aware of how his shape might change as he gets fitter, especially near the end of a run-up to a ride. If he develops back or girth sores during a competition, he will be eliminated. To prevent this happening, numnahs or saddle pads should allow plenty of air to circulate; also, when washing the horse down, ensure he is well dried before the saddle and girth go back on. Equally sweat will cause sores, so must be removed. Note that oversized pads will inhibit loss of heat by normal means and so will increase the horse's body temperature – so watch out for this. Natural fibres are best for cooling and comfort.

Cooling Down

Ensure that adequate cooling methods are used. Do not cover the horse's body with towels: always wash and remove the water, and re-wash. Walk the horse if he is agitated, and wash at the same time. Not returning to

the same spot to re-wash also seems to help stressed horses. Re-check his temperature regularly, and do not abandon the cooling procedure until it is sufficiently lowered. Stand the horse under trees or in the shade to help keep him cool.

Look After Yourself!

Don't forget *you* can become dehydrated very easily, so it is important that *you* drink enough, too. And this should consist not just of water, but an electrolyte/sports drink to help replace lost body salts. Mental concentration and physical ability are all affected by dehydration, so at recognised stops have *your* drink ready, to replace lost fluids; otherwise you will compromise your horse by being both mentally and physically under-charged.

Suppling Exercises

Massage: Use this as routine procedure during the horse's day-to-day regime to help maintain muscle tone and ease of movement:

- Pre-exercise – such as a schooling session – to aid muscle development and physical function.
- 1–3 hours after exercise and competition, to reduce the effects of exercise.
- To promote relaxation in the stressed environment at a competition.

Dehydration and overheating can cause many physical and mental problems, for you as well as your horse. Look after yourself as your horse needs you to be up to the job

Areas to concentrate on regularly are the limbs, back and hindquarters (see p102–11).

Suppling exercises: Do these before any exercise session to warm up and loosen soft tissues and joints. Use ridden suppling exercises, for example lateral work and circles, two to three times a week to improve co-ordination and flexibility.

Stretching exercises: Do these only when the horse is warmed up, either at the end of an exercise session, or after 20 mins warm-up. Concentrate on the shoulder (see p.130) and the hindquarters (see p.132).

At checkpoints: Use palpatory hands examination on head and neck to calm and relax the horse. Use a static, resting hand, with light pressure 1–2/10 on areas of restriction or tension. *Hold* for 20 seconds: if the horse responds by dropping his head and looking sleepy, maintain at 1–2/10 pressure until he has had enough (he will wake up or move away when this happens).

The late Reiner Klimke performing in competition: pure athleticism combined with perfect harmony

SPECIFIC REGIMES FOR SPECIALIST DISCIPLINES

For most of us, dressage is simply schooling the horse to make him safe and pleasurable to ride; when performed seriously, and particularly at its highest level, it is a demonstration of pure athleticism and perfect harmony between rider and horse. The overall picture is of elegance.

For a dressage horse to be able to perform correctly he needs to have a rounded vertebral column and good back and stomach muscles. A good horse expends a great deal of energy in performing these more advanced movements, and this increases with the technical difficulty and the degree of collection required. The more transitions there are, the more effort is required from the horse; and the greater the degree of collection demanded, the greater is the degree of flexion required in the hip, stifle and hock joints as increasingly the hindquarters must carry the horse's bodyweight and not just propel him forwards. As the hindquarters learn to bear this weight, the hip, stifles and hocks must flex to an

increasingly great degree to absorb concussion, and extend as they push off the ground. For a horse to be able to work well in collection he has to be physically mature enough to cope, and it will take many months to build up the muscular strength and endurance of the appropriate muscles. To improve his strength, hill work and gymnastic jumping, together with his routine schooling in the dressage movements, will all help a horse at medium level and upwards.

TRAINING
Dressage Movements
Use plenty of transitions, and practise each dressage movement repeatedly, being very careful to ride correctly at all times to obtain the best possible movement. If you do not, you risk strengthening other muscle groups; also if you continue to work the horse when he is tired, other muscles will come into play

to help out the fatigued ones, and you will end up with well-developed muscle where it is not wanted for optimum performance.

Muscle strength is increased by using the movements themselves, but without overdoing them, and by taking plenty of rest intervals in between, when ridden suppling exercises may be used. Sufficient repetitions that increase the workload progressively will stimulate changes in the muscle fibres and encourage structural muscle changes. It is therefore important to start with work periods that are relatively short, with longer rest intervals in between, and not repeated too many times, and build up progressively to longer work periods with shorter rest intervals, increasing the number of repetitions according to the horse's improving fitness.

Hill Work

Working a dressage horse on a slope introduces variety to his training regime, and can significantly improve his physique. By working at slow speeds up and down gradual inclines at varying gaits you will encourage engagement of the hindquarters. For horses working at novice up to medium level, working across a slope in a wide zigzag at walk and slow trot will help to strengthen the low back and hindquarters; this will prepare them for more vigorous demands in their schooling work. At more advanced levels, working down a slope performing dressage movements as you go will increase further the flexion potential of the horse's hind-leg joints. Transitions and halts up and down a slope will improve his strength and balance.

Gymnastic Jumping

Gymnastic jumping can often achieve increased hip, stifle and hock joint movement even more effectively than the repetition of dressage movements on the flat. For example, from medium level upwards you need to

Hillwork encourages engagement of the hindquarters

improve the shortening and lengthening performance of the extensor muscles of the hindquarters, and a grid of small bounce fences will exercise this particular group of muscles with most effect. It also helps to develop neck and back suppleness. To increase the difficulty of the exercise, vary the number of fences and the number of repetitions, not the height – you want to increase muscle endurance, besides which the higher the fence, the greater the risk of strain or injury.

Gymnastic jumping improves strength and suppleness and is good mental activity, too

147

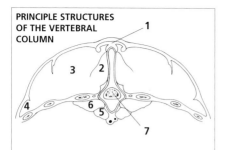

PRINCIPLE STRUCTURES OF THE VERTEBRAL COLUMN

1: Supraspinosus ligament
2: Transversospinalis group
3: Longissimus dorsi
4: Iliocostalis
5: Psoas minor
6: Psoas major
7: Vertebral canal and contents

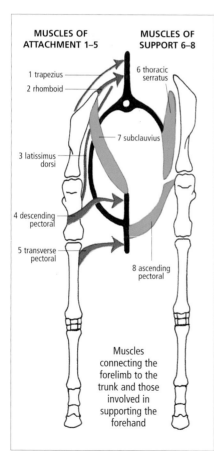

MUSCLES OF ATTACHMENT 1–5

1 trapezius
2 rhomboid
3 latissimus dorsi
4 descending pectoral
5 transverse pectoral

MUSCLES OF SUPPORT 6–8

6 thoracic serratus
7 subclauvius
8 ascending pectoral

Muscles connecting the forelimb to the trunk and those involved in supporting the forehand

Ridden Suppling Exercises

A ridden suppling programme for the dressage horse is intended to improve the roundness and flexibility of the vertebral column (left), and to increase the range of movement in all directions of the shoulder and hip. The benefits of suppling will be to increase the horse's suppleness and therefore the bend through his body, and so improve

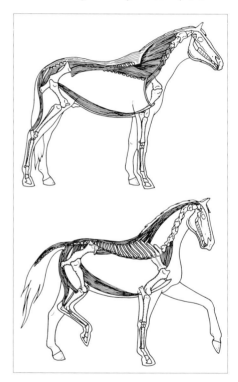

The 'ring of muscles' in a standing horse (top) and in action (above). Functioning together correctly, the muscles work to accentuate the curves in the vertebral column and therefore allow maximum movement potential. The abdominal muscles concentrically contract to provide lift and support. This causes shortening of the abdomen and increases the top line roundness and suppleness.

Concentric contraction of the long muscles of head and neck causes the neck to be raised and the lumbosacral and theraco lumbar area to flex, promoting hindleg engagement.

the quality of movement in his lateral work: it should help to increase his length of stride, and increase the degree with which he can cross his limbs. The front legs have no bony connection to the body, and enhancing the range of scapula and shoulder movement is crucial in this (far left, bottom).

For engagement of the hindquarters in canter the horse must have good flexion of the lumbosacral joint: this will rotate the hindquarters forwards and engage the hind legs. Flexion of the hip, stifle and hock joints is also necessary for this engagement. The hip joints also need to be free to move inwards and outwards to allow the hind legs to step sideways. To this end, ridden suppling exercises should include turns, circles, lateral work and frequent transitions, all of which movements will encourage bending and rotation in the thoracic region of the spine, and maximise shoulder and hindquarter flexibility.

It is very important to work the horse at the appropriate degree of engagement for his stage of training. Furthermore during each schooling session do not forget to allow him to stretch long and low in between exercises – and make sure that the top of his neck stretches, too. This should be done regularly. Suppling exercises can also be done using trotting poles: at walk and trot this promotes active bending of the limb joints, and it is an exercise that can be used right from the beginning for any dressage horse in training.

Allow the horse to stretch down between exercises to allow the muscles to lengthen. This reduces fatigue and maximises function

MANAGEMENT AND CARE

We have discussed that dressage horses need other forms of training to help them mentally and physically – hill work, hacking out over different terrain, and gymnastic jumping will help maximise development, and prevent over-development of some muscle groups.

Turning them out is also very important, to help them relax and to stimulate normal function. Furthermore warming the horse up in hand, and doing suppling exercises will reduce the risk of injuries, particularly if he tends to be excitable in his work. You might follow a massage programme such as this:

Novice level:

1 Pre-exercise	Shoulders, withers and hindquarters (see p.95, 96, 105)
2 Suppling exercises	All
3 Stretching exercises	(10 mins warm-up) hind leg, shoulders (see p.130, 132)
4 Post-exercise massage	Neck and back 1–3 hours after exercise (see p.90, 103)

Medium level upwards:

1 Pre-exercise	Hindquarters (see p.105)
2 Suppling exercise	All
3 Stretching	Shoulders, neck, hindquarters (see p.130, 126, 132)
4 Post-exercise massage	Upper neck 1–3 hours afterwards (see p.90) and hindquarters (p.105)

Driving Horses

SPECIFIC REGIMES FOR SPECIALIST DISCIPLINES

Driving is now a very broad area of equestrianism, whether it is pursued for pleasure, or competitively. There are many different classes and disciplines, from simple turn-out to driving trials, and therefore many different types of horse and pony are in demand. Scurry ponies must race at speed though a course of cones – the fastest wins – whereas ponies driven for pleasure may never have to negotiate anything more demanding than the gentle camber of the road. However, the one thing they have in common is that they pull a carriage, and as such are susceptible to similar physical demands in varying amounts.

The ultimate in speed and suppleness: scurry ponies at full stretch

The format of a driving trials is similar to that of eventing: it takes place over three to four days and consists of a dressage test, a marathon (speed and endurance) and cone driving. The dressage phase tests suppleness and obedience; the marathon, fitness and stamina, and accuracy through various hazards; and the cone-driving, fitness, obedience and suppleness – and after a strenuous marathon phase, this is indeed quite a considerable test. The marathon is always energetically demanding, over often difficult terrain that may vary from sticky and deep, to rugged and hard. The main gait is trot, but through the hazards the horse will sometimes canter, which requires extra effort.

TRAINING

As a general rule, all driving horses should take some form of exercise other than being driven to help promote flexibility and strength, and to reduce the concussive effects on their limbs. Other exercise methods might include the following:

- Loose schooling
- Lungeing
- Long-reining
- Water treadmill (1–3 times a week)
- Swimming
- Ridden exercise
- Ground work, ie TTOUCH & TEAM, a method of training that utilises specific body movements and handling skills to stimulate normal movements.
- Pirelli, a method of handling and training that is based on the horse's natural instincts and lifestyle.
- The Monty Roberts technique.

Under Saddle and Driving

To improve cardiovascular fitness, it is a good idea to work the horse on hills, increasing the workload by increasing the distance, and the degree of the slope, and the number of times you go up and down it. When descending, be careful to control the horse's speed, balancing him well at trot to reduce the stress on his

joints; otherwise you risk damage to the bones and cartilage and other supporting structures such as tendon and ligaments.

Under saddle you can perform all the usual schooling movements to maintain and improve shoulder and hindquarter flexibility; and increase fitness by doing faster work. Again, hill work, and in particular working across an incline, will help strengthen the low back muscles that support the pelvis. For the pony or horse that cannot be ridden, long-reining and lungeing can be used as an alternative suppling exercise.

One way to build up the horse's strength for pulling the carriage in competition is to progressively increase the weight of the carriage, then use terrain of increasing difficulty. For driven suppling exercises, use circles, initially large and slow, then smaller and faster.

When training a driving horse for trials, give him time to recover on the days in between intensive training. Avoid excessive concussion on the limbs and joints at all times, and work out an alternative exercise programme for him, rather than hammering along the roads.

The cross-country phase of competitive driving demands stamina, teamwork and flexibility

CARE AND MANAGEMENT

One general point that might be made here is that you should try to move horse positions in the carriage each time you go out in it, to avoid problems of one-sidedness developing in the horse.

Suppling Exercises	
Pre-exercise massage:	Hindquarters
Pre-exercise suppling exercises:	All
Post-exercise stretches:	Hindquarters: do at least 10 mins exercise before performing these.
Post-exercise massage:	Shoulders, neck, quarters: 1–3 hours after exercise.
Refer to:	Stretches p.126 Suppling exercises p.114 Massage p.90

151

The Western Horse

The Western horse is used for pleasure and for competition. He is trained to be responsive to the slightest pressure from the heels, and to obey a subtle rein contact. He is often ridden for long periods at a time, and is sure-footed and strong – he must work on varying terrain, and be quick to adapt and react. As a sport, Western riding has developed to incorporate many different disciplines: halter classes, showmanship, Western pleasure, horsemanship, trail class, Western riding, reining and cutting.

The *reining* horse has to be particularly athletic, so a correct conformation is important: he should be short-coupled, with a short muscular neck, and flexible joints for speed and agility. He will perform 360° spins at speed, do lead changes and 180° pivots on his hocks, and roll-backs in both directions. He has to be able to do a sliding stop where he gallops and shifts all his weight to his haunches; the front legs at this point should keep moving to make the stop as long as possible. He does all this in 1–2 minutes, and receives marks for his performance. He will be performing moderate to high intensity exercise, with high energy expenditure due to the stop and turns and sudden changes of speed.

TRAINING

The Western horse needs to be very supple to maintain the overall quality of the reining performance. He will incur the risk of injury if he is compensating for lack of range of movement on the tight turns. He needs great strength to be able to control and perform the sliding stops and roll-backs. Often these classes are started when the horse is just three years old, so he

Western horses need to give a sudden burst of speed as they are released from the pen

The sliding stop demands both strength and athleticism as the horse must pull himself in with his front legs with his weight on his haunches

needs to commence a programme from two years old upwards. This is not always in his best interests, however, because if he is not given time to develop the strength of the supporting structures – hoofs, tendons, ligaments, bone – he will be particularly prone to injury.

Ridden Suppling Exercises

For strength, the horse must work off his hindquarters. He needs propulsive muscle power, so hill work, loping up and down gradual inclines, will engage his back end. To engage the back end he also needs good flexibility of the lumbosacral and hip joints: riding circles at slow speeds, then gradual curves, and progressing to smaller circles at faster speeds, will improve flexibility. To be able to do spins and roll-backs, the horse must have a good range of movement, particularly in his spine; and on turns through the shoulders, he must cross his front legs on a spin – so the scapulae and shoulder must be as flexible as possible.

MANAGEMENT AND CARE

Pay particular attention to saddle fitting and pads. These are very important due to the design of the Western saddle which can cause back pain from undue pressure. It is tremendously important to have good foot nutrition and foot biomechanics to prolong the horse's soundness.

Finally, the Western horse needs correct dental care and the correct bit position.

Suppling Exercises

Pre-exercise massage:	Shoulder, hindquarters.
Suppling exercises:	Do all before exercise.
Stretching exercises:	Do 10 mins warm-up at least twice a day: shoulders, hindquarters.
Post-exercise relaxation massage:	Shoulders, hindquarters, 1–3 hours after exercise.
Refer to pp. 90, 126, 114	

Polo Ponies

Typically the polo pony is a fairly small, athletic horse. He has to carry a large person at speeds of up to 30–40mph in short bursts, and during the game must accelerate and decelerate and change direction very quickly indeed. The energy required to cope with these rapid muscle changes and the forces applied to them is tremendous; and ponies must also cope with being bumped and moved sideways as one player 'rides off' another in pursuit of the ball. As a result they are generally very tough and stoical, with a high pain threshold.

Polo is a game that consists of a series of chukkas, one chukka lasting for seven minutes, and ponies are always kitted out (out-fitted) in what appears to be a fearsome arrangement of boots and bridleware. Leg boots and overreach boots are essential to protect them against the impact and interference injuries that result to the limbs; and because they must stop, start and turn quickly, they are nearly always ridden in a gag snaffle or a pelham together with a standing martingale and a variety of nosebands.

TRAINING

During exercise the polo pony experiences high intensity activity, and this will create a build-up of lactic acid in the muscles; his training must therefore be structured to help his body cope with this process. Strength training is important for inproving acceleration and speed, and this will also help increase the pony's strength in a ride-off. Furthermore by following a proper strength programme you will raise his chances of staying sound by strengthening the lower limb structures.

Hill work is most useful in a polo pony's training programme, and should be structured so that the gradient is progressively increased, and also the speed that he goes up it; the more mature and fitter ponies should be able to work

Polo ponies must be strong, bearing in mind the frame of the rider, the speed at which they travel and the impact in a 'ride off'

very quickly on a slight to moderate uphill gradient. This work will help to develop their propulsive muscles. To develop 'ride off' ability the pony should be taught the technique at walk, then he can progress to doing it at trot, and finally at canter. To be able to 'ride off' another pony effectively he will need strength and momentum, and also a lot of confidence.

Ridden Suppling Exercises

To enhance athleticism and reduce the risk of injury it is very important that a polo pony's daily exercise routine moves the joints through their full range of capability. Ridden suppling exercises should therefore involve circles and lateral work, and these should be performed initially at slow speeds to increase neck and spinal flexibility; in particular this will help the shoulders and hips. Suppling and stretching exercises also help to promote relaxation and decrease post-exercise muscular soreness.

Polo ponies are allowed only one minute's warm-up on the field, and no time at all for warming down. This is a most unfortunate situation for the pony, because if he has to play two chukkas and is not cooled down correctly he will probably be suffering fatigue symptoms and associated problems due to the high levels of lactate acid produced as a result of the energy expended during play. Ideally the warm-up should consist of at least ten minutes of forward movements to increase the temperature of the muscles. It should include circles for suppleness, initially fairly large and slow and progressing to smaller and faster ones, and in the last few minutes, sharp turns and abrupt transitions to mimic the requirements of the competition – this will ensure that the muscles, tendons and ligaments are fully stretched. After each chukka the pony should be given a proper warm-down to ensure lactate removal and prevent muscle soreness and fatigue – ideally this would be five minutes of relaxed trotting in big circles. And once the pony is back in the lines, gentle suppling exercises of the limbs will also help those who have old muscle restrictions.

MANAGEMENT AND CARE

Most of the time that a polo pony spends in play, he spends with his head in the air, and such a head carriage is invariably detrimental to his neck and back muscles. Nor is he helped by the fact that his rider is generally an adult who is

Boots can help protect against injury

too heavy for him. Thus the least that can be done to help him in training and in his day-to-day care is to encourage a more natural posture. This might include schooling movements to stretch his topline and encourage lengthening – this will help to prevent over-development of the under-side of his neck muscles, and should also help to keep him sound. Loose schooling will promote suppleness without stressing his back with the weight and pressure of a saddle or roller. In the stable, give him his feed off the floor: like this his neck and back describe the vertebral bow that is his natural posture.

In my experience, saddles, in the world of polo, are often not maintained very well, nor are they fitted by an experienced saddler. A well fitting saddle is very important, as the pony is normally carrying a large adult, and it is imperative that the rider's weight is distributed evenly. The saddle must *not* compromise the pony's flexibility and athleticism by causing impingement and muscle damage.

Nutrition

Many polo ponies are roughed off very quickly at the end of the season and turned out to fend for themselves – another situation that could really be improved. Correct adherence to nutritional needs during the pony's resting months, and regular dental care, all help in maintaining bodily condition, and thereby promote a long and useful life.

Exercise Therapy

Pre-exercise massage:	Shoulders, hindquarters.
Pre-exercise suppling exercises:	Shoulders, hindquarters.
Stretching exercises after warm-up of 10 minutes:	Neck, shoulders, spinal.
Massage post-exercise:	Neck, shoulders, hindquarters, 1–3 hours after exercise.
Maintenance in season:	Massage general body 3 days before competing
Refer to:	Suppling exercises p.118 Stretching p.126 Massage p.88 Nutrition p.56

155

The Aged Horse

The old companion retired in his field will be an ideal candidate for massage and suppling exercises. Massage performed either on specific areas, or all over, will help to maintain pain-free mobility, and will promote relaxation and comfort. And once the weather gets colder and he starts to stiffen up, he will almost certainly find relaxation massage very soothing and effective. Sometimes as movement becomes more cautious he might miss his footing, and in these circumstances massage on his limbs will help sensory and motor function.

The suppling exercises can be modified slightly so they are performed very slowly and low to the ground. Always start on the horse's better limb and leave the stiffer one to the end.

General maintenance of the older horse is very important, particularly of his feet and teeth. Often because these retired horses are turned out and not being exercised, we wrongly believe that nature will see them right. Regular trimming will help to prevent cracks in the hoof, and will help their general comfort and prevent problems.

MASSAGE AREAS

Neck: Aids spinal mobility.
Limbs: Improves co-ordination and awareness.
Abdomen: Aids spinal mobility and eases the digestion.
Hindquarters: Helps the horse in getting up and down.

SUPPLING EXERCISE PROGRAMME

These exercises can be done in the field if it has a good, level surface. Also the horse must be standing well, with his head up.

The Fore Limbs

Step 1: Pick the foot up as if you were cleaning it out.
Step 2: Describe a circle with the limb from foot and fetlock – keep it small and slow **(1)**. Do x 5 in each direction,

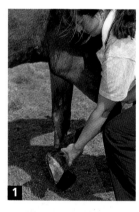

keeping the foot low to the ground. If the horse is comfortable, proceed to the next step.

Step 3: Move limb away from side of body, and repeat step 2. If comfortable, do step 4.

Step 4: Move limb halfway up neck level, still with the foot only just off the ground **(2)**.

3

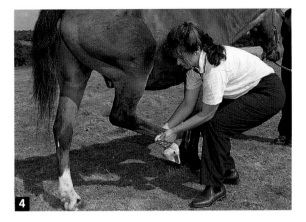

4

The Hind Limbs

The procedure for the hind limbs is similar:

Step 1: Pick up the foot.

Step 2: Describe small circles low to ground **(3)**, x 5 each way.

Step 3: Move limb slightly away from side and describe small, slow circles, x 5 each way.

Step 4: Move limb towards stomach, keeping low to ground **(4)**; describe small, slow circles x 5 in and x 5 out.

5

Step 5: Walk towards the tail with limb **(5)**: at point of resistance stop and draw a circle x 5 one way and x 5 the other.

Repeat on the opposite limb.

Tail Exercises

Step 1: Stand to one side and grasp top of tail firmly **(6)**.

6

Step 2: Move tail slowly in a circular motion from top of tail: go x 5 clockwise and x 5 anti-clockwise **(7)**.

Step 3: Bring tail slowly across fully to one side and hold

3 secs. Then go to opposite side and hold 3 secs.

Step 4: Make a question mark shape using both hands **(8)**. Hold 3 secs.

Step 5: Gently replace down.

7

8

Useful Addresses and Publications

ORGANISATIONS

Tellington TTouch Equine
Awareness Method and
Tellington TTouch
www.lindatellingtonjones.com
E-mail: info@tteam-touch.com
        Sarahfisher@msn.com
In the USA:
PO Box 3793
Santa Fe, NM 87501
Tel: 800-854-TEAM
www.TellingtonTouch.com
E-mail: TTEAM@compuserve.com

Parelli Natural Horse•Man•Ship
Tel: 01435 872556
USA tel: 800-642-3335
www.parelli.com

Intelligent Horsemanship
Association (Monty Roberts and
Kelly Marks)
P.O. Box 2035
Marlborough
Wiltshire SN8 2TL
Tel: 01488 72772
www.montyroberts.co.uk
In the USA
Tel: 888-U2-MONTY
www.montyroberts.com

Society of
Master Saddlers (UK) Ltd
Kettles Farm
Mickfield, Stowmarket
Suffolk IP14 6BY
Tel: 01449 711642

Society of Teachers of the
Alexander Technique
20 London House
266 Fulham Road
London SW10 9EL
Tel: 020 7351 0828
In the USA:
AMSAT
Tel: 800-473-0620
www.alexandertech.org

Association of Chartered
Physiotherapists in Animal
Therapy
Secretary: Joyce Verey
Tel: 01962 863801
www.acpat.org.uk

American Holistic Veterinary
Medical Association
Tel: 410-569-0795
www.altvetmed.com
E-mail:
AHVMA@compuserve.com

MAGAZINES

The Horse
www.thehorse.com
The Equestrian Directory (annual)
www.beta-uk.org

EQUUS
www.equusmagazine.com

COURSES

Equissage
P.O. Box 447
Round Hill
VA 20141
Tel: 800-843-0224,
Fax 540-338-5567
www.equissage.com

Animal Therapy
Harestock Stud
Kennel Lane
Littleton
Winchester
Hampshire
England SO22 6PT
www.animaltherapy.co.uk
E-mail:
amanda@animalphysio.co.uk

Bibliography

The Life of Horses
Jane Holderness Roddam
Mitchell Beazley (UK), Hungry Minds (US)

Equine Massage – A Practical Guide
Jean Pierre Houdebaight
Ringpress Books Limited (UK), Hungry Minds (US)

Sports Injuries – A Self-help Guide
Vivian Grisgogono
John Murray (Publishers) Ltd (UK), Trafalgar
Square (US)

Therapeutic Massage
Elizabeth Holey & Eileen Cook
W.B. Saunders Company Ltd

Saddle Fitting
An Allen Photographic Guide
Kay Humphries
Robert Hale (UK), Trafalgar Square (US)

Index

159

INDEX

All photographs by Bob Langrish except the following:
Author's collection: pp 7, 8, 45(ctr&btm), 130(btm rt), 139, 146
Abbey Saddlery: pp 59, 60(top rt)
Buxactic Ltd: p59(btm rt)
Kit Houghton: pp 60(top rt), 64(top l to r)
Balance International: p65
Bob Atkins: p138(top)
Colin Vogel: p140

All artworks by Maggie Raynor except the following:
Author: p23
Samantha Elmhurst: p148(top & btm rt)

Artworks on pp50–2 are based on illustrations that appear in 'Optimising the Performance of the Sports Horse Through Welfare' published by Nixon & Marshall Veterinary Surgeons, Maids Moreton, Buckinghamshire